How
Minority Status
Affects Fertility

HOW MINORITY STATUS AFFECTS FERTILITY

Asian Groups in Canada

Shivalingappa S. Halli

Contributions in Ethnic Studies, Number 18

Greenwood Press
New York • Westport, Connecticut • London

Library of Congress Cataloging-in-Publication Data

Halli, Shivalingappa S., 1952-
   How minority status affects fertility.

   (Contributions in ethnic studies, ISSN 0196-7088 ;
no. 18)
   Bibliography: p.
   Includes index.
   1. Fertility, Human—Canada.   2. Asians—Canada—
Population.   I. Title.   II. Series.
HB939.H35   1987   304.6'32   86-19453
ISBN 0-313-25534-2 (lib. bdg. : alk. paper)

British Library Cataloguing in Publication Data is available.

Library of Congress Catalog Card Number: 86-19453
ISBN: 0-313-25534-2
ISSN: 0196-7088

First published in 1987

Greenwood Press, Inc.
88 Post Road West, Westport, Connecticut 06881

Printed in the United States of America

The paper used in this book complies with the
Permanent Paper Standard issued by the National
Information Standards Organization (Z39.48-1984).

10   9   8   7   6   5   4   3   2   1

IN MEMORY OF MY PARENTS

Contents

Figures

Tables

Series Foreword

The Contributions in Ethnic Studies series focuses upon the problems that arise when people with different cultures and goals come together and interact productively or tragically. The modes of adjustment or conflict are various, but usually one group dominates or attempts to dominate the other. Eventually some accommodation is reached: the process is likely to be long and, for the weaker group, painful. No one scholarly discipline monopolizes the research necessary to comprehend these intergroup relations. The emerging analysis, consequently, is of interest to historians, social scientists, psychologists, psychiatrists, and scholars in communication studies.

Before World War II Asians in Canada, specifically the Chinese and then the Japanese in British Columbia, suffered the kinds of economic and social discriminations endured frequently by racially distinctive minority groups. Thereafter their status and that of East Indians throughout Canada have been ameliorated; for example, they have been admitted to Canadian citizenship. After reviewing the historical developments, the author of this study concentrates upon one intriguing, interdisciplinary problem: Is the fertility rate of the Asian groups in Canada different from that of other Canadians and, if so, how can the differential rates be explained?

To answer these questions, unpublished data from the 1971 Canadian census and other sources are examined in great statistical detail. On the immediate surface it is evident that the birth rates of the Asian groups fluctuate with a number of factors, such as the mothers' ages, the duration of the marriage, the educational level of the parents, various "historical factors," and ethnicity. The basic problem then becomes whether the differences in fertility rates of the Japanese and Chinese Canadians, concerning whom adequate quantitative information is available, do or do not remain similar when their distinctive demographic are statistically controlled or analyzed.

That problem is explored in depth by considering current theories and findings concerning the scholarly literature on fertility both in Canada and the United States. The author is next able to provide objective indices of the ascribed and perceived sociopolitical statuses of these Chinese and Japanese Canadians. Together with other indices, a convincing generalization emerges concerning the probable effects of ethnicity and demographic factors upon fertility. Relevant statistical methods provide a tentative but compelling solution to one of the many possible consequences of the interaction between a majority group and its submerged ethnic minorities. This study, therefore, offers a methodology and hypotheses potentially applicable wherever the perpetuation of an ethnic group through its progeny is at the focus of scholarly or political attention.

Leonard W. Doob

Preface

Traditionally, differences in family size between groups or subpopulations were thought to be a function of socio-economic variations in the compositions of these groups. But even when differences in these characteristics are eliminated through equalitarian social change or statistically through standardization or some form of control, the differences in family size across subpopulations may not disappear. This has given rise to the development of the minority group status hypothesis as an alternative or complimentary explanation. This alternative explanation indicates that even when groups are similar on socio-economic characteristics, minority group membership will continue to exert an independent effect on fertility.

The review of the literature on minority group status and fertility relationship indicates an inconsistency in results. The cause of this inconsistency lies in the way the minority -status hypothesis is used in the literature. Much of the past research on ethnic fertility differentials focuses on socio-economic factors in an attempt to explain observed variations in fertility between majority and minority population; the remaining variances are attributed to the minority status of the ethnic groups. This study questions the validity of this residual explanation as a net minority status effect on fertility. In the past, the support or non-support for the hypothesis was often based on how the groups have been classified. That is, the hypothesis is based on poor conceptualization and lack of direct measurements of the concepts involved. A careful classification of minority groups is necessary in order to avoid inconsistent patterns of minority group fertility across minority groups relative to the majority group. For the social-psychological interpretation to be convincing it would be necessary to measure these attributes directly. Essentially this task has been undertaken in this study.

Another focus of this research has been the study of Asian ethnic fertility differentials in the multi-ethnic society of Canada based on the 1971 Census of Canada. The extent of fertility differentials as well as possible sources of variation in fertility behaviour of the major Asian ethnic groups-Chinese, Japanese, East Indian, and others-are studied. Ethnic fertility differentials are examined in their socio-economic and historical context. It is found that each of these ethnic groups have experienced inequality of treatment and discrimination in areas such as employment and services. Also documented are differences in socio-economic characteristics that are shown to be related to fertility differentials. Finally, the re-conceptualized minority group status hypothesis has been used to explain the family size differences of Chinese and Japanese groups in Canada.

A number of people have provided various forms of assistance in writing this book. I wish to thank them: Messers. T. R. Balakrishnan, K. G. Basavarajappa, R. P. Beaujot, T. K. Burch, E. Ebanks, C. F.Grindstaff, C. Hirschman, W. E. Kalbach, W. Marshall, E. T. Pryor, S. Ramcharan, F. Trovato and A. Wister. I would also like to thank the anonymous referee for Greenwood Press for his/her very useful comments on the previous version. I especially want to thank Mrs. Mildred Vasan, Ms. Julia Marothy and Mr. W. Neenan for their valuable guidance and other assistance in the preparation of this book. I owe special thanks to my wife, Rohini, and daughter, Priyanka, for their co-operation. Last, but not the least, I am more than thankful to Mrs. Nancy Smith for her help in preparing the camera ready copy.

How
Minority Status
Affects Fertility

1

Asian Ethnic Fertility in Canada:
An Application of the
Minority Group Status Hypothesis

Canada is known as a country of immigrants of different ethnic
groups from various parts of the world. Out of the total
population of 21.6 million in 1971, 3.3 million, or 15.1
percent, were born outside of Canada; over 1 million had
arrived during the preceding decade, and another 1.3 million
had settled during the post-war years, from 1946 to 1961.
Roughly four million Canadians enumerated in the 1971 census
were born to immigrant parents. Those who were native born to
Canadian-born parents amounted to the remaining two-thirds of
the population (Richmond and Kalbach, 1980). Based on 1981
census figures, Pryor and Norris (1983) state that Canada's
immigrants are coming from different countries than they did
in the past. During the 1978 to 1981 period, European immigration dropped below 30 percent while nearly 44 percent came
from Asia. During the decade 1971-1981, the total
foreign-born population increased 17 percent while the number
of persons born in Asia increased 228 percent (Pryor and
Norris, 1983). This multi-culturalism is highly conducive to
social and demographic differentiation along ethnic dimensions
(Vallee et al., 1956; Porter, 1965; Reitz, 1980). Consequently, much recent research in Canadian demography
emphasizes the importance of the ethnic effect in various
demographic components (Henripin, 1972; Beaujot, 1975;
Balakrishnan, 1976; Richmond and Kalbach, 1980; Krauter
and Davis, 1978; Trovato and Burch, 1980; Trovato and Halli,
1983; Basavarajappa and Halli, 1984).
    Classical studies of immigration relied heavily on the
concepts of assimilation and integration. Generally, the
linguistic and cultural assimilation of immigrants has been
distinguished from the structural aspects which include the
demographic, geographic, and socio-economic dimensions
(Richmond and Kalbach, 1980). The process of assimilation has
been represented as a progressive convergence by the immigrant
population toward the characteristics of the native-born. Any

deviation from this phenomenon demonstrates the varying degrees of ethnic and subcultural influences.

The history of Asian-origin people in Canada is more than a century old. Yet there is no systematic study of these immigrant groups. It would be interesting to investigate why immigrants from Asia have consistently been omitted or neglected. The study of Asian immigrants in Canada is important not only from an academic point of view but also from socio-economic and political points of view. Such an investigation would result in a thorough understanding of the differences between the cultures, their social and reproductive behaviour, and institutions. This would help to promote a better relationship between immigrants and native residents and make possible more effective inter-group relations and cooperation. More important, such a study would help to prepare the receiving people for a better acceptance of immigrants by knowing how and why their cultures are different so that any existing prejudices are minimized. As Beck (1980) points out, the results of Asian ethnic studies "can contribute both to policy formation and to the pride, identity and well-being of Canadian society at large." (p. 2)

An historical review shows that the Canadian association with Asia is somewhat "special" and "different," particularly with Japan (Norris, 1948). It can also be noted that Chinese were among the earliest non-white immigrants to enter Canada with the opening of the Cariboo goldfields, after their previous experience in the California gold rush of 1849 (Anderson and Frideres, 1980). However, the flow of Asian immigrants had been slow till the late 1960s due to restrictive immigration policies. After the liberalization of such policies in 1967, arrivals from Asian sources increased from 6 to 23 percent of the total arrivals during the period 1966 to 1973, while the proportion of immigrants arriving from European countries declined from 76 to 39 percent (Anderson and Frideres, 1980). In recognition of this fact, the Canadian government helped to form, in 1969, the Canadian Asian Studies Association, which organized special sessions at the Learned Societies Meetings of 1977 and 1978. The results of these meetings produced an edited book containing twenty-five research papers (Ujimoto and Hirabayashi, 1980). Though this work stands as a milestone in Asian ethnic studies in Canada, it is confined to a description of the adjustment experience, community structures, and organizations. Other aspects covered in the study are "official" reaction by the host community, official immigration decisions, current human rights policies, and pending immigration legislation. None of the papers included in the book analyze the demographic processes. The long history of Asians in Canada, the special aspects of immigration policy affecting Asian groups, as well as the proportion of Asians in recent immigration, point to the need for a detailed study of the demography of this particular group. The present study is a partial fulfillment of such an objective.

In this book, an attempt is made to investigate the family size differences among Asian ethnic groups in Canada based on specially obtained data from Statistics Canada. The intent is not only to study the extent of fertility differentials alone but also to assemble possible sources of variation in fertility behaviour of these groups. Rindfuss and Sweet (1977) advocate that the study of fertility differentials should take into account the social, cultural, and historical contexts. For this reason, we will begin our study by presenting some of the socio-historical background of Asian-origin groups in Canada. We hope any differences in the groups' historical experience and background characteristics will help us to understand the fertility pattern and family size variation of these groups. Moreover, an attempt will be made to investigate how the minority status hypothesis, originally formulated mainly in the context of the United States, might be used to explain differentials in Asian ethnic fertility in Canada. This perspective posits that minority group status per se affects fertility independent of social, economic, and demographic factors. The underlying assumption of this hypothesis is that the social-psychological insecurities associated with minority status are reflected in their fertility behaviour.

Goldscheider and Uhlenberg in 1969 developed the minority group status hypothesis as an alternative when they found the social characteristics and particularized theology propositions had failed to account for complete fertility variation of ethnic groups. They argued that once the discrepancies in social characteristics were eliminated and no longer operate to differentiate fertility behaviour and attitudes, the residual fertility of minority groups may result from the insecurities associated with minority status. This approach has received significant research attention, at least in the United States. However, application of the hypothesis outside of the United States has been quite limited, and no one has made an attempt to apply it to the study of Asian ethnic fertility. In this study an attempt will be made to use the hypothesis to explain the fertility variation of Asian groups in Canada and to try to resolve some of the issues left unclear by the above authors--such as how and under what conditions minority group status either depresses or increases fertility and what dimensions of minority group identification influence fertility behaviour. Before we apply the revised theory to the present context, the study of related socio-economic and demographic charactertistics will be presented, and independent effects of age and marriage duration will be assessed using a decomposition procedure.

1.1 THE RELEVANCE OF ETHNICITY IN FERTILITY STUDIES

Ethnic differentiation is present in one form or another in most societies. Berelson (1978) indicated four bases of such differentiation:

> Race: a common biological heritage involving certain, usually permanent, physical distinctions readily visible; religion: a common and distinct system of worship; nationality: a common or regional origin usually characterized by distinctive linguistic patterns. Often, perhaps typically, such differences are reinforced by residential segregation: that is, ethnic groups tend to live together in regions of a country or sections of a city and thus reinforce their ethnic character. (p. 74)

The relevance of ethnicity in fertility analysis has been studied, and the relationship between ethnicity and fertility has been documented historically in North America. In the case of Canada, researchers have found fertility differentials by the various ethnic groups (Hurd, 1937; Henripin, 1972; Kalbach and McVey, 1979). In recent years there are two conflicting orientations about the relevance of ethnicity in fertility analysis: one group argues that in modern days the ethnic origin concept is a relic with little behavioural significance (Sly, 1970; Johnson, 1979). The other side of the argument is that ethnicity continues to show its impact on human behaviour in general and on fertility in particular (Beaujot, 1975; Kalbach, 1970).

The fundamental question that has been raised by Balakrishnan et al., (1979) is about the definition of ethnicity--is it an historical ancestry or is it more a personal identification, regardless of the ancestry or passage of time? This is a valid question given the ambiguous definitions of the related key concepts. A variety of terms have been used more or less interchangeably with ethnic group--race, culture, subculture, folk, people, nation, nationality, minority group, ethnic minority, ethno-linguistic group, ethno-religious group (Anderson and Frideres, 1980). The definition of ethnicity is multifaceted, and the term has been confusing because of the diverse explicit and implicit meanings attached to it.

It is difficult, if not impossible, to come up with a complete definition of ethnicity. Often an ethnic group is a minority group (at least numerically), and it is also a racial, cultural, or religious group. If the ethnic group is a minority group, a complete definition ought to consider the following additional criteria: (1) small size relative to the total societal population (Blalock, 1966); (2) a relatively clearly defined subculture and separate pattern of social interaction (Petersen, 1968; Elliot, 1971); (3) an historical pattern of opposition from and discrimination by the dominant population (Petersen, 1968); and (4) a membership determined by ascription through a "socially invented 'rule of descent'" (Wagley and Harris, 1959: 10). In this study, for the sake of simplicity, the concept "ethnic group" refers to one's "ethnic or cultural background traced through the father's side" (Richmond and Kalbach, 1980: 31). We will reserve discussion of the term "minority group" for chapter 4, section 4.3.

The study of ethnic fertility differentials is important in the Canadian context, particularly, in view of the large numbers of immigrants. This point of view is emphasized in Beaujot et al. (1977):

> The analysis of fertility differences among ethnic or religious groups is important from both a practical and theoretical point of view. Such differences in levels of reproduction have obvious consequences on the future proportional representation of those socio-cultural groups. This is particularly relevant for those groups that contribute large numbers of immigrants because their share in the total population is affected by both their migration rate and their relative level of reproduction. (p. 1)

Other Canadian researchers have also speculated that ethnicity is an important explanatory variable and sometimes a better predictor than other social and economic characteristics in fertility studies. According to Balakrishnan et al. (1975),

> The lower fertility of foreign-born women and the differences among them according to ethnicity is an important finding. . . . Given the importance of immigration and the ethnic factor in Canadian fertility it would be admissible in future fertility research to give the variable greater consideration. (p. 34)

There are other reasons as well why ethnicity is important in the study of fertility differentials. First, ethnic affiliation does have different socio-economic and political consequences for the populations of many nations. Traditionally, it has affected access to political and economic power and, in turn, has generated division rather than unity. Also, it is extremely useful in the analysis of assimilation processes. It may not be out of place to quote Glazer and Moynihan (1975) who argue that ethnicity has not lost its importance in behavioural research over the years, as was predicted by social scientists in the early 1950s.

> [T]he long-expected and predicted decline of ethnicity, the fuller acculturation of the

> white ethnic groups, seems once again
> delayed--as it was by World War I, World War
> II, and the Cold War--and by now one suspects,
> if something expected keeps on failing to
> happen, that there may be more reasons than
> accident that explain why ethnicity and ethnic
> identity continue to persist. (p. 23)

1.2 THEORETICAL BACKGROUND

In attempting to explain differential fertility levels among Asian ethnic groups, the concept of minority group status has been used to show how members of ethnic groups with a low minority group status suffer from feelings of "insecurity," which in turn affects their fertility behaviour. The recent research in this area of enquiry has shown that there is no consistent pattern of minority group fertility (across minority groups) relative to the majority (Goldscheider and Uhlenberg, 1969; Sly, 1970; Roberts and Lee, 1974; Ritchey, 1975; Jiobu and Marshall, 1977; Johnson, 1979). Part of the problem is lack of conceptual clarification and failure to measure the key theoretical variables. The problem arises when one moves from the aggregate categorization of minority group status to the individual or family unit level. Minority group status to a large degree depends on ethnic identity, and ethnic identity entails more than just membership. Unless a unified theory is conceptualised and attributes are measured, it is difficult to account for minority fertility variation, whether above average or below.

In this book, we will try to distinguish between the two explanations, one explaining reduced minority fertility and the other explaining high minority fertility and thereby reconceptualize the theory. The revision of the theory would encompass elements of both macro and micro levels of analysis to contain the dimensions such as group norms and values, as well as individual decision-making regarding family size and fertility based on economic, biological, and psychological factors. Both macro and micro types of factors regarding fertility control and family size influence the "intermediate" variables, which in turn shape fertility levels. The latter type of variables intervene between the organization of society on the one hand and fertility on the other. According to Goldscheider (1971), the social organization framework which includes social, structural, cultural, and normative variables (i.e., macro-level factors), social-psychological and personality components (i.e., micro-level variables), and the intermediate mechanism themselves.

It is useful to briefly describe the theoretical background for the above-mentioned three types of factors (micro, macro, and intermediate). This will provide a summary of relevant fertility literature, from which we will later draw when we expand on the minority status and ethnic fertility relationship.

Micro Level

With respect to individual decision-making processes, the two principal sources are Easterlin (1975) and Fishbein (1972). Their perspectives seem most appropriate for micro-level analysis since Easterlin accounts mostly for economic factors whereas Fishbein emphasizes psychological dimensions. Thus, the two theories in conjunction could provide us with a workable micro theory of fertility.

Economic Factors. According to this perspective, fertility behaviour is a result of household choice in which resources are weighed against preferences for children as opposed to other consumer "goods." Potential income, tastes, and costs are therefore key variables. The three factors elaborated by Easterlin in his micro economic theory are (1) C_d, the demand for children if fertility regulation were costless, (2) C_n, the potential output of children if no conscious effort were made to control fertility, and (3) the cost of fertility regulation.

The demand variable is determined by income (potential income) of the household, the cost of children relative to other goals, and the tastes of the couple or subjective preferences vis-a-vis material goods as mentioned below. The household balances tastes and preferences for children as compared to other consumer durables such as cars, television sets, or other expensive goods. The constraints imposed by the price of children, relative to other goods, and by the couple's income determine their decision with regard to how many children they will want to have. Thus, the greater the taste for children, the more they will want, but the more expensive are children, the fewer they will want. Concerning income, the economists prefer to think in terms of permanent income (i.e., the potential amount the couple will earn in their lifetime). It has been found that the higher the income, the lower the family size. This is due to the output value attached to children and the development of tastes for expensive goods. The couple opts to have few children in order to ensure maximum quality (i.e., high education, etc.). Moreover, with an increase in income, there is an increase in the demand for more expensive and luxurious consumer durables. Thus, the household reaches an equilibrium point so that psychic and material satisfactions are maximized.

The potential output-variable depends on natural fertility or the number of births in the absence of intentional limitation to control births. Thus, natural fertility must depend also on biological factors such as sterility and ill health and also on cultural norms regarding abstinance, including taboos regarding contraception, menstruation, and the post-partum period.

The costs of fertility regulation include two types: psychic or subjective costs and market costs, which are related to time and money to learn and pay for contraceptive methods. Thus, the higher the cost, the lower the accessability of fertility control.

Easterlin's framework outlines the effect of rationality working through the three factors mentioned above. It is possible, then, that an increase in income may have the effect of either increasing or reducing fertility, depending on the couple's tastes for children and material goods and their desire for quality of children. The question which needs to be raised at this point is, how is a couple's motivation to reduce or increase fertility formed, considering the three variables discussed? The potential output and the demand for children jointly determine the motivation of fertility regulation.

If Cn (potential output of children) is less than Cd (demand for children), there is no desire to limit fertility. In this situation, knowledge and availability of contraception would not significantly alter overall fertility. What would cause variations in fertility, however, are such factors as frequency of intercourse, physical illness, or infant mortality plus intermediate factors to be discussed later. This sort of situation is encountered in many developing and underdeveloped nations. For example, Poffenberger and Poffenberger (1975) describe the cultural incentives on Indian women to have high fertility since status and authority are often determined by the number of children one has.

In contrast, if Cn (potential output) is greater than Cd (demand), parents would be motivated to control fertility since they would encounter the prospect of unwanted births. The extent to which fertility control will be adopted depends on the cost (psychic and material) of fertility control and on the motivation to limit fertility. Thus, the greater the motivation to limit fertility and the lower the cost and availability, the closer would the actual number of children correspond to the desired number of children. Of course, the opposite would tend to lead to greater levels of unwanted or unplanned fertility.

In summing up Easterlin's economic theory, children are viewed as consumer "goods" which are weighed against other material and non-material "goods" (e.g. leisure, privacy, etc.) by couples who try to maximize satisfaction with their available resources. As mentioned, this implies costs (material such as income restraint or cost of contraception and psychic costs) and tastes plus biological factors.

Psychological Factors Influencing Fertility Behaviour. In Easterlin's theory there is mention of motivation and tastes which may be best conceived as more psychological than economic variables. However, the question remains: What psychological and personality variables influence people's motivation to either have high or low fertility? It becomes necessary to briefly discuss and thus integrate personal factors in a micro-level theory of fertility.

In regard to personal factors, Hoffman and Hoffman (1973) elaborate the function and needs children serve for parents. They list nine "values" of which we will briefly mention four: (1) children are a means of achieving adult recognition and social approval; (2) children are a means of expanding the self; (3) children serve as moral conformity to social expectations since childbearing involves giving up one's own interest for the sake of another person, community, religious tradition, and norms supporting impulse inhibition; and (4) children can be viewed as a source of stimulation, fun, creativity, accomplishment, and power for the parents. Rearing children provides parents with the opportunity to feel that they have created a child who will eventually grow up and perhaps provide them with vicarious satisfaction through his/her accomplishments. The authors describe these personal values of children in great detail; for our purposes, the few examples provided are sufficient. Fishbein (1972) speaks of other personality factors such as authoritarianism as being influential in fertility behaviour. The authoritarian personality is much more likely to ascribe to normative behaviour than the non-authoritarian. Similarly, it is possible to conceive of personality factors such as introversion-extroversion and psychoanalytic personality factors as also influencing fertility through subconscious motivations anywhere from resolution of Oedipal and Elektra complexes to the life instinct.

In determinants of motivation and behaviour, Fishbein's model focuses on the relationship between behavioural intentions and actual behaviour relative to family planning. There are basically two interrelated components: (1) the individual's beliefs about the consequences of performing a behaviour and his/her subjective judgment of the "probability" or "improbability" that his/her performance of the behaviour will lead to certain consequences and (2) the concept of "normative beliefs," or the perceived expected performance desired by one's reference group under a given circumstance. Therefore, the individual's beliefs about the norms governing the behaviour being considered and the motivation to comply or not to comply with the norms become important in the decision process to adopt family planning techniques or not.

Individual behaviour is determined by the relative weight of each component. For example, if the normative component is stronger than the individual's beliefs about an act's consequences, the likelihood of any behaviour violating the norms is low. In contrast, if the individual's assessment of the consequence for acting contrary to the norms is favourable (subjectively), the probability of acting is high.

Thus an interplay between economic and psychological factors is influenced to an extent by cultural norms. For example, in Easterlin's theory, the proposition that if Cn is lower than Cd (if potential output is lower than demand for children), there is no desire to limit fertility in a society where the norm is low fertility. According to Fishbein's theory, individuals not limiting fertility have assessed the consequences as favourable even though in essence they are violating the social norm. The point is that economic and psychological factors are interrelated when people consciously decide on the number of children they want.

Intermediate Factors

These factors mediate between fertility on one hand and the social organizational determinants of fertility on the other. The social organizational determinants include stratification variables, family structure variables, technological factors, non-familial institutions, and other characteristics of social and economic organizations (Freedman, 1963). These variables influence actual behaviour and final cumulative fertility through intermediate variables, such as age at entry into unions, extent of celibacy and period of exposure to risk, contraceptive use, extent of infecundity, and the practice of abortion. Goldscheider (1971) argues that whatever changes may be observed in fertility patterns over time and whatever societal fertility differences may occur at any point in time must be a direct function of variables associated with sexual intercourse, conception, and gestation. The interplay of these "intermediate" variables is responsible for fertility levels, trends, and variations. Recent development of a simple equation to measure the relative contribution of these variables by Bongaarts and Potter (1983) has made even more attractive the use of intermediate variables in fertility research.

Davis and Blake (1956) provide the original discussion of intermediate variables. There are basically four divisions which contain subclassifications under each one of the four. We will not state every one of these since it is really not necessary for our purposes. Hawthorn (1970) discusses the Davis and Blake formulation and concentrates on the most important which are (1) those factors governing the formation and dissolution of unions in the reproductive period such as age of entry into sexual unions, proportion of women never entering unions, divorce, separation, desertion, or death; (2) frequency and exposure to intercourse within unions such as sexual taboos, periods of abstinance due to norms regarding post-partum activity; (3) factors affecting conception such as norms regarding use and non-use of contraceptives and accessibility of fertility control. Therefore, societies with varying norms and expectations regarding these factors will experience different levels of fertility. For example, Stycos (1968) documents the phenomenon of "consensual unions" in Latin America, wherein "common law" and "legal marriages" tend

Thus, Davis implicitly describes an aggregate event with basic psychological principles such as reward, costs or punishment, motivation and frustration. Davis implies, in his article, that once a particular behaviour is initiated due to some stimulus (i.e., mobility opportunities, change in aspirations, and the conscious curtailment of family size) and it proves to have rewarding consequences for the individual, it becomes reinforced. Homans (1974) would argue that this is, in fact, the process of how social institutions originate and become reinforced in society, beginning at the level of basic psychological impulses. The development of social structure and social exchange can thus be reduced to the basic principles which constitute the character of man. The economists place much more emphasis on rationality. They do not concern themselves with lower level psychological mechanisms. They analyse social exchange from the point of view that man is end-seeking and is involved in rational decisions in the attempt to reach an equilibrium between maximum utility and maximum satisfaction. Thus, social structures emerge from economic exchange among people. Society is viewed as emanating from economic exchange, with rationality being the fundamental principle of behaviour. Blau (1964), for example, concerns himself with the same issue as Homans and argues that complex social structures may be derived from the basic social exchange process. Homans however is content to explain this only by psychology; Blau goes further to explore the economic base of social action. Thus, while economic motives are a function of psychological needs, economic exchange is the basis of social structure.

It is important to note that human reproduction is also a central part of the decision-making process. However, individual decisions are made within the context of social structure. Social norms and pressures are components of human decision making. Namboodiri (1980) argues that the individual is not free to ignore norms completely. It is important that some minimum resource allocation be made to effect some minimum level of adherence to norms: "Norms are there to be adhered to, no matter what the perceived price tag is." (p. 85)

Robinson and Harbison (1980) have made an attempt to present an integrated model of fertility. Their schematic representation is reproduced here (Figure 1.1). This figure includes factors appropriate to fertility decisions on the individual, family, and social levels. It is easy to see that different forces--economic, cultural, social, and psychological--all interact in determining the actual fertility decisions of couples. More specifically they explain the following:

Psychological variables shape the individual's reaction to external forces and stimuli; sociological variables shape the group's reaction to and control over individual behaviour, while the whole process proceeds in a roughly economic cost-benefit "expectations" framework. In any given situation, or for any given birth parity, it is quite possible that one set of forces may dominate and overshadow the others. Thus, the parity one birth decision may be strongly affected by the fundamental psychological "values" while economic factors become more important for higher parities. Social "norms" may dominate individual utilities in societies with very little margin for error ecologically speaking, whereas in a less confining environmental situation, "norms" may be freely ignored and rapidly lose meaning. (pp. 228-29)

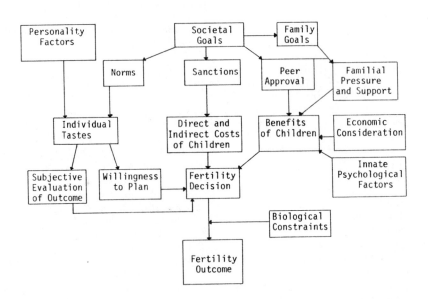

FIGURE 1.1: An Integrated Fertility Model of Robinson and Harbison (1980:226)

The more simplified version of the above model, which can be easily operationalized, is that of Fishbein's (1972) value-expectancy perspective. Basically, that model assumes that individuals are faced with two possibly opposing alternatives: (1) to do as one pleases under certain conditions or (2) to do as the individual perceives his reference group (i.e., ethnic group), would approve. Thus the model is

$$BI = (\sum_{i=1}^{n} Bi\ Ai)\ W_1 + (\sum_{i=1}^{m} NBi\ MCi)\ W_2$$

where:

    BI is the behavioural intention to perform an act
       (i.e., to have a child)

    Bi is the belief that performance of the act will
       lead to some consequence

    Ai represents the value of performing the act to the
    individual

    NBi is the perception of how acceptable the act is
       to the reference group

    MCi refers to the individual's motivation to comply
       with his/her reference groups' norms about an
       act

    W_1 and W_2 are empirical weights of the components in

the equation.

The component on the left is an additudinal one; the one on the right represents the normative component.

The argument of Robinson and Harbison (1980) may be even more appealing if we apply Fishbein's model to an empirical situation. One such example is to explain the experience of French Canada with regard to fertility patterns of past and present, from an individualist-rational view. It may be argued that in the past, during the period of high fertility, French Canadians were responding predominantly in a normative fashion. Given the fact that the French were once the dominant group in Canada and subsequently became a minority, strong norms for high fertility may have developed as a response to their situation. Thus, at the individual level, the component ($\sum NBi\ MCi$) may have had greater weight than the attitudinal one ($\sum Bi\ Ai$). People observed the norm of high fertility and were highly motivated to do so since such behaviour was thought to engender positive consequences for the group (i.e., political strength).

In recent times, the lower fertility of French Canadians may be explained in terms of a shift in the weight of the two components. Rationality in contemporary society is translated into low fertility in order to ensure personal--not group--maximization by the group members. Thus Fishbein's model suggests that ($\sum Bi\ Ai$) has the greater empirical weight as opposed to ($\sum NBi\ MCi$).

The lesson to be learned from the above discussion in the context of minority status and fertility is that there is a need for a two-edged unified theory of minority status and fertility. To understand ethnic fertility behaviour, it is useful to recognize that the several approaches interact. From the above discussions, it is clear that there is a strong overlap among the cultural, economic, social and psychological approaches. Failure to recognize this in the past research on minority status and fertility has led to inconsistent conclusions. Individual tastes are influenced by personal, psychological, and group norms. Group norms are developed by groups to achieve their own objectives. On the other hand, couples' motivations do not always follow group taste, norms, or calculation. This leads to the conclusion, mentioned earlier, that individuals are faced with two possibly opposing alternatives: (1) to do as one pleases under certain conditions or (2) to do as the individual perceives his reference group would approve. In any given situation it is quite possible that the force that dominates will become responsible for one's fertility outcome.

1.3 THE PLAN OF ANALYSIS AND PRESENTATION

Although Statistics Canada collects detailed information on Asian ethnic groups, for many characteristics the data are published only for the Chinese and Japanese. Perhaps one of the reasons for a lack of demographic research on Asian groups in Canada is the non-availability of published data. However, it is possible to obtain special tabulations on a cost-recovery basis from Statistics Canada. We have used this opportunity, and hence the data used for the study are special unpublished cross tabulations from the 1971 census. We will also use data from the 1971 public use sample tapes, one in one hundred individual files.

As already indicated the objective of the thesis is to study the extent of fertility differentials as well as possible sources of variation in fertility behaviour of Asian ethnic groups. The theoretical perspective used for explaining the differential fertility among the groups is the minority group status hypothesis. Unfortunately, there has been no consensus regarding the validity of this thesis to explain the fertility variation of sub-populations. Therefore, we need to revise this theory based on the comments and criticism that are available before we can apply it to the Asians. It is possible that this theory can overlap at least in some respect with some of the other theoretical perspectives used in fertility research. Because of this, we briefly reviewed the relevant theoretical background on fertility research with the hope that we may be able to improve the minority group status hypothesis by drawing upon the theoretical background already presented.

The minority group status hypothesis becomes relevant only when social, cultural, and historical factors are unable to account for complete fertility variation (Rindfuss, 1980). It has been demonstrated that changes in fertility behaviour that have been found within social, economic, and racial groups cannot be accounted for by changes in the population composition, and their explanation must be linked to historical events (Rindfuss et al., 1978). Hence, we will begin in chapter 2 with the historical review of Asian origin groups in Canada. This should provide the foundation of an understanding of the background of Asian ethnic groups in terms of their historical experience in Canada. Knowledge of this may provide us with an explanation of variation in fertility behaviour between the dominant group in Canada and the Asian minority. Apart from historical background, chapter 2 also contains other characteristics of Asian-origin groups such as rural-urban residence, demographic characteristics, and socio-economic disparities. This will enhance our understanding of the family size differences of Asian ethnic groups.

The main purpose of chapter 3 is to present Asian ethnic fertility differentials based on the unpublished data. The variation of family size differences with age and age at marriage are discussed. Fertility indices such as parity progression ratios and a life table approach are used. A decomposition procedure is employed to study the relative importance of age and marriage duration. Finally, the effect of nativity in the fertility of Asian groups is assessed. (In chapters 2 and 3 the focus is on the Asian groups themselves; a comparison of Asian groups to the majority society is included in chapter 5.)

Having established the Asian ethnic family size differences in chapter 3, we want to examine how the pattern of ethnic differences in fertility varies with some indicators of socio-economic status when other demographic factors are taken into account. If socio-economic differences do not account fully for Asian ethnic fertility differentials, the minority group status hypothesis may become an alternative explanation. The use of this alternative explanation for black-white differences in fertility in the United States has been the subject of considerable debate among researchers. There have been numerous comments and criticisms regarding an application of the minority group status hypothesis to explain ethnic fertility differentials. Hence, in chapter 4, an attempt is made to re-examine the minority group status hypothesis as a theoretical framework for investigating ethnic differences in fertility. This begins with a review of the literature on this area of enquiry. In the process of assessing the past research, the possible inadequacies and shortcomings of the theory are identified. Finally, an attempt is made to present a reformulation of the theory, including a discussion of the new concepts and their operationalization.

The revised theory is applied to the study of Asian ethnic fertility differentials in chapter 5. Thus, the revised theory is not tested in the broader context of Canadian ethnic fertility differentials but only in the context of Asian ethnic differences in family sizes. We first obtain proxi measures of key theoretical concepts of the theory. In order to know how minority -group membership operates independently to affect fertility, the British majority group is considered as a reference category. The method of analysis and interpretation is based on the type of data available to us.

Finally, in chapter 6, we summarize the results of our investigation and discuss the implications of our findings for future ethnic fertility research.

2
Historical and Background Characteristics of Asians

The objective of this chapter is twofold. One is to present a brief historical perspective on Asian immigration to help us understand their cultures, social behaviour, and institutions. This will also provide the necessary historical background to examine the recent immigrants from Asia to Canada. Not much has been written about these immigrants, but we will present whatever historical information is readily available. The study period is the modern era; thus we will not consider the prehistoric immigration of the native population. For the sake of convenience, the period is made up of two phases: pre-World War II and post-World War II. Between these phases the pace of migration varied considerably. Though social and economic factors affected the rate of migration, the most dominant factor was government regulations (Beaujot and McQuillan, 1982). Hence, during this discussion, frequent references are made to the actions taken by the Canadian government to encourage or regulate the flow of immigrants.

The second objective of this chapter is to document the Asian ethnic differences with regard to the socio-economic and demographic characteristics that might be related to their fertility differentials. The assumption is that the more modern an ethnic group is in their background characteristics, the more modern they are in their fertility behaviour. For example, lower family sizes may be associated with higher education, higher income, urban background, and greater female labour force participation. It may not always be possible to find a systematic relationship between fertility and background characteristics due to the confounding effects of 18 differential age composition and age at marriage, which are associated with the background variables.

The tables presented in this chapter regarding background characteristics are determined by the type of data available. These characteristics are basically socio-economic and demographic variables such as age at the time of the 1971 census, type of residence, period of immigration, family income, occupation, education, work status, religion, and the language spoken most often at home. The tables that are constructed for these background characteristics are derived from special cross tabulations obtained from Statistics Canada, based on unpublished 1971 data.

2.1   PRE-WORLD WAR II PERIOD

Chinese Immigrants

The history of Oriental immigrants begins with the arrival of Chinese gold miners in British Columbia in 1858 (Boggs, 1923). This first group of Chinese immigrants did not come directly from China but from the United States. When gold was discovered in the Caribou district and along the Fraser River, miners from California arrived, including as many as two thousand Chinese (Cheng, 1931). Cheng reports that there were 2,500 Chinese in 1863 and they were hired in all kinds of business--in the fisheries, the sawmills, and on the farms; they also served as domestic servants, cooks, and laundrymen.

However, anti-Chinese activities were frequent as some of the big companies in British Columbia used the Chinese as a weapon to settle the disputes with white labourers (Boggs, 1923). When the mining boom came to an end and the depression took hold in 1866, Chinese immigrants left the mine fields and moved to other occupations. As a consequence, the competition between the immigrants and local white workers increased. Since the Chinese were prepared to work for lower wages than the whites, partly because as single people they had fewer needs and a lower cost of living, they did not face problems in securing employment. The continuous increase of the Chinese immigrants and their attitudes toward employment were seen as decreasing the opportunities for white people. The reaction from the white workers was antagonistic. The anti-Oriental movement was supported by some of the members of the British Columbia Legislative Assembly (Woodsworth, 1937). On February 26, 1872, John Robson, a member of the legislature, made a motion that a "humble address be presented to his Excellency the lieutenant-governor, praying that a bill may be sent down to this House, during its present session, providing for the imposition of a per capita tax of fifty dollars a head per annum, upon all Chinese within the province" (Cheng, 1931:38). Robson was concerned that the Chinese, instead of the native labourers, would benefit from the forthcoming $30 million project of the Canadian Pacific Railway. Opponents felt that white labour was unobtainable and that more Asian immigrants would be needed to work for the early realization of the Canadian dream--the transcontinental railway line construction. The Dominion government also wanted the early completion of the railway for commercial and military purposes (Woodsworth, 1937). The railway contractors took advantage of the situation and brought in cheap and efficient labourers from China, Hong Kong, and the United States--over 15,000 between 1881 and 1885 (Boggs, 1926).

Following a series of anti-Chinese representations to Ottawa to restrict Chinese immigration, a Royal commission was established to study the pros and cons of the Chinese immigration (see Outlook, 1906). The commission recognized the contribution of the immigrant group in developing the mining, fishing, and agricultural resources of British Columbia. The commission did not agree with some of the members of Parliament from British Columbia regarding total exclusion of the Chinese immigrants. The commission members argued that the possibility of trade development between Canada and China meant that Parliament should try to maintain the interest of the whole Dominion, instead of the unreasoning prejudice of a small group in British Columbia (Cheng, 1931). However, to satisfy some of the British Columbian politicians and workers, a bill was passed in 1885 to regulate Chinese immigration. According to this new bill, every Chinese entering Canada would pay a head tax of $50, of which the province would receive one quarter. This became the first anti-Chinese law in Canada (see Round Table, 1923).

The law proved to be quite effective, at least in the beginning. During 1885, before the bill became law on August 20, nearly 4,000 Chinese entered British Columbia. From August 1885 to January 31, 1886, only 235 entered Canada. This was possible only because, when the bill was being discussed in Parliament, the Chinese in Canada warned their friends and relatives in China not to come (Cheng, 1931). Cheng documents that during the same period, 688 Chinese left Canada, so the Chinese population actually decreased. However, during the period from January 1886 to December 1889, more than 10,000 Chinese entered Canada, at an average of not less than 1200 per annum. Not all of them paid a head tax, as 888 were exempted because they were merchants and students, and some of them were returning to Canada.

Groups of people in British Columbia were still not happy about the law on Chinese immigration, and they wanted a complete exclusion of Chinese immigrants. Due to continuous agitation of these groups, the British Columbia legislature took a step to regulate Chinese employment. The government inserted a clause in an 1886 act, which provided that no Chinese should be employed, either directly or indirectly, in any contract offered by the British Columbia government (Cheng, 1931). In case of violation of the act, a fine of $25 was imposed for every Chinese employed. In addition, the British Columbia legislature asked the Dominion government to increase the head tax to $200. Though not immediately, the Dominion increased the per capita tax to $100 in 1902 (Round Table, 1923). On the other hand, British Columbia inserted a clause in an 1896 act to the effect that no Asian should be entitled to vote at any municipal or provincial election. It also passed a labour regulation act in 1898, which provided that no Oriental immigrant should be used in connection with the works authorized by the province, but the Dominion government disallowed the act because it violated treaty rights. Instead, the Dominion increased the head tax to $500 in 1903, of which one half went to the province (see Round Table, 1923).

The people of British Columbia were pleased about the increase in the head tax, and they were sure that it was almost impossible for any Chinese to enter Canada by paying $500 as a head tax. Just before the act came into force, nearly 4,719 Chinese entered Canada during 1903. During the period from July 1904 to June 1907, there was a sudden drop in immigration; only 121 paid the tax and entered the country (Cheng, 1931). The people of British Columbia thought they had "solved" the problem of Chinese immigration, but they were wrong. Between July 1907 and March 1908, the number of Chinese immigrants increased to 1,482 (Cheng, 1931). Ironically, the reasons for this sudden increase after a gap of three and a half years lies in the head tax itself, which was meant to stop the Chinese. The Royal commission appointed in 1908 by the Dominion government to investigate the method by which oriental labourers had been introduced to Canada found that Canadian business organizations had come forward to pay advance wages so that Chinese would come and work for them. Business organizations had recognized the qualities of Chinese labourers such as their extraordinary aptitude for grinding toil, cheerfulness, lack of aggressive action, and submissiveness. Moreover, the resident Chinese also helped their relatives and friends by loaning them the head tax (Cheng, 1931).

When the anti-Chinese union in British Columbia realized that the tax did not attain the aim for which it was imposed, anti-Oriental riots occurred in Vancouver in September 1907 (Shaw, 1924). This riot was different from previous ones. Cheng (1931) reports:

> Some excited men in the crowd suggested that the Oriental quarters be attacked, and the mob at once responded. A thousand strong men marched down to the Chinese quarters, shouting like madmen. The few policemen on the street were powerless to stop them. The Chinese, taken by surprise, fled into the inner chambers of their shops. All the windows were broken by the mob and some shops suffered great damage. Then they went to the Japanese quarters and did the same thing. (p. 76)

This violent action against the immigrants was condemned by many citizens of British Columbia, as well as the Victoria Colonist, a paper which had been anti-Chinese since 1872. The government made an investigation of the loss to the Chinese immigrants, and $25,990 was paid by the Dominion, including legal expenses (Shaw, 1924). The Dominion government also became stricter in admitting Chinese immigrants into Canada, yet there was a steady increase until the beginning of World War I. The detailed account of oriental immigration to Canada during the period from 1886 to 1971 is shown in Table 2.1.

For about two years after the riots of 1907, Chinese immigration jumped suddenly to 4,515 during the fiscal year of 1910-1911, and this trend continued. In 1911-1912, more than 6,000 immigrants of Chinese origin entered Canada, and in 1912-1913 as many as 7,078 Chinese entered Canada (Cheng, 1931). The local employers started misusing the large number of easily available immigrants. In August 1913 the coal miners in Vancouver went on strike, but the employers used Chinese labourers to work in the mines as strike breakers. The angry strikers became violent, and damage was done not only to the companies but also to Chinese workers and shops (Cheng, 1931). However, the British Columbia government paid the loss that occurred to the Chinese immigrants during these riots as the federal government had done earlier (Woodsworth, 1937).

The situation was reversed during World War I, when many Oriental immigrants were allowed to enter Canada because of manpower shortages, and in fact Oriental immigrants served as soldiers with the Canadian troops. But this did not last long. When a period of depression and unemployment followed the war, new hostilities toward Orientals started in British Columbia. The Monthly Labour Review (1927) documented that there were already around 50,000 Chinese in British Columbia alone. The Dominion government was concerned about this huge population of Chinese immigrants, and the most dramatic step was taken in May 1923, when the government passed legislation excluding Chinese immigrants from Canada. China reacted strongly against the discriminatory legislation, and those feelings were expressed in the China Review, May 1923, as follows:

> In an era which is characterized by a tendency on the part of the civilized countries to promote friendliness and understanding among all people, to effect progress by friendly co-operation and by refraining from activities tending to engender ill feeling and animosity, the bill on the subject of Chinese immigration into Canada, now pending enactment by the Canadian Legislature, may be said to be an anachronism. It is incongruous with the spirit of a better order, and particularly repugnant to what is known as the British sense of fair play. There seems little reason for, and surely no justice in, attempting the passage of a bill which is calculated to exclude Chinese citizens from the privileges of residence in Canada. Moreover, its enactment is bound to work economic injury to Canada both directly and indirectly . . . only one motive is possible behind any effort to exclude them, and that one is race prejudice. The world has little to

TABLE 2.1
Record of Oriental Immigration to Canada 1886 to 1971

Year	Chinese	Japanese	Year	Chinese	Japanese
1886	212	-	1929	-	194
1887	124	-	1930	-	205
1888	290	-	1931	-	195
1889	892	-	1932	1	115
1890	1,166	-	1933	2	105
1891	2,125	-	1934	-	93
1892	3,282	-	1935	-	83
1893	2,258	-	1936	1	103
1894	2,109	-	1937	-	139
1895	1,462	-	1938	-	46
1896	1,786	-	1939	-	36
1897	2,471	691	1940	-	45
1898	2,192	1,189	1941	-	1
1899	4,402	1,875	1942	-	1
1900	4,257	9,033	1943	-	-
1901	2,544	1,125	1944	-	-
1902	3,587	165	1945	1	-
1903	5,329	185	1946	7	3
1904	4,847	97	1947	25	3
1905	77	354	1948	114	8
1906	168	1,922	1949	1,036	13
1907	291	2,042	1950	1,746	13
1908	2,234	7,601	1951	2,708	3
1909	2,106	495	1952	2,320	7
1910	2,302	271	1953	1,936	49
1911	5,320	437	1954	1,958	73
1912	6,581	765	1955	2,602	102
1913	7,445	724	1956	2,103	124
1914	5,512	856	1957	1,686	185
1915	1,258	592	1958	2,630	193
1916	89	401	1959	2,586	197
1917	393	648	1960	1,402	169
1918	769	883	1961	894	126
1919	4,333	1,178	1962	876	154
1920	544	711	1963	1,571	199
1921	2,435	532	1964	3,210	163
1922	1,746	471	1965	5,234	219
1923	711	369	1966	5,178	535
1924	624	448	1967*	4,044	858
1925	-	421	1968*	5,259	628
1926	-	475	1969*	5,272	698
1927	3	478	1970*	3,465	785
1928	1	446	1971*	2,877	815

Source: Tien-Fang Cheng (1931), Oriental Immigration in Canada, Table
I of Appendix 2, Shanghai: The Commerical Press Ltd., for the years
1886 to 1924.

Annual Reports of Citizenship and Immigration. Department of Citizenship and Immigration, Ottawa, for the years 1925 to 1966.

*Figures refer to the country of citizenship instead of ethnic origin
and are taken from the Quarterly Immigration Bulletin, Department of
Citizenship and Immigration, Ottawa.

boast of if race prejudice that works injustice and
feeds hatred plays any role in the relations among
civilized nations. (p. 209)

The Chinese associations in Canada also strongly condemned the
bill and passed a resolution choosing July 1 as a humiliation
day.

Japanese Immigrants

The story of the early Japanese immigrants is quite
different, mainly because they were few in number (Young and
Reid, 1938).   Before 1900, there were fewer than 4,000
Japanese, who came mostly from the United States.   But the
number of immigrants began to increase rapidly at the
beginning of the present century.   Table 2.1 provides the
account of Japanese immigration from 1897 to 1971.   It is
clear from the table that during the five-year period from
1896 to 1901, nearly 14,000 Japanese arrived in Canada.   But
the 1901 census shows that only 4,738 Japanese were residing
in Canada.   Cheng (1931) attributes this discrepancy to the
fact that the majority of the Japanese who entered Canada
during 1896 to 1901 were ultimately destined for the United
States, not for Canada.

Anti-Japanese activities started in British Columbia,
including in the British Columbia Legislature, during the
early 1900s, but there was no support for these activities
from the Dominion government.   By 1900, Japan had already
achieved power and prestige in international affairs.   The
friendship between Great Britain and Japan was growing, and in
fact Great Britain had an alliance with Japan in 1902.   It
thus became important for Great Britain to ensure that Japan
was not offended by Canada through its immigration policies.
Although British Columbia passed legislation to keep Japanese
immigrants out, Great Britain put pressure on the Canadian
government to reverse the offending legislation (see Round
Table, 1923; Outlook, 1906).   Japanese companies took full
advantage of this opportunity and brought in huge numbers of
Japanese workers.   By 1907 there were 18,000 residents of
Japanese origin in Canada, and another 7,600 arrived in the
province during 1908.

British Columbia was now feeling the burden of Japanese
immigrants.   This feeling, together with the news that large
numbers of Asian immigrants including Hindus were coming in,
was responsible for the riots that occurred in Vancouver on
September 7, 1907 (Shaw, 1924).   During these riots, fifty-six
Japanese stores were severely damaged and several Japanese
were badly hurt.   (These riots were described in the previous
section and are not discussed here.)   The riots against the
Japanese were quite embarrassing to the Dominion government,
as Great Britain protested to the Canadian government about
the incidents.   The Canadian government promised to do full

justice to the Japanese damaged. A commission was formed under the chairmanship of Mr. MacKenzie King, then deputy minister of labour, to investigate the incident. The losses and damages were assessed by the commission, and the loss was paid by the government of Canada to the Japanese (Shaw, 1924).

The Canadian government wanted to make sure that riots would not occur again and hence sent the minister of labour, Mr. Lemieux, to Japan to discuss the regulation of Japanese immigration to Canada (Whiteley, 1931). After a month's discussion with Japanese officials, Mr. Lemieux reached a so-called "gentlemen's agreement" on December 23, 1907. The essence of the agreement read as follows:

> [A]lthough the existing treaty between Japan and Canada absolutely guarantees to Japanese subjects full liberty to enter, travel, and reside in any part of the Dominion of Canada, yet it is not the intention of the imperial government to insist upon the complete enjoyment of the rights and privileges guaranteed by those stipulations when that would involve disregard of special conditions which may prevail in Canada from time to time. (Cheng, 1931: 123)

This agreement satisfied both the parties, and they were happy that the Japanese immigration problem was settled.

After the gentlemen's agreement, Japanese immigration structure was changed. Before the agreement, Japanese immigration, like Chinese, consisted mostly of adult males. By virtue of the agreement, domestic and agricultural labourers could come to Canada with their wives and children. The Japanese (non-married males) who were already in Canada were able to get married by importing their potential brides from Japan. In this way, many Japanese women were brought into Canada, and in fact the number of Japanese women exceeded that of men by 1912 (Cheng, 1931). Cheng states that there were 4,738 Japanese in 1901, all of whom were males. By 1921, there were 10,520 males and 5,348 females; out of these, 2,279 males and 2,055 females were born in Canada. This indicates that for the first two decades of the present century, the increase of Japanese male and female immigrants was almost equal--3,503 males and 3,069 females (Cheng, 1931).

The increase of Japanese women in Canada and their high fertility posed a problem to the Canadian government. This time it was not a problem of immigration but of reproduction. There were also serious concerns among many members of Parliament regarding a potential monopoly of the fishing and farming industries by the Japanese. The people of British Columbia were seriously concerned about the Japanese immigrants who were enjoying special privileges. The Chinese population was not now considered the major concern since the Dominion government had already enacted restrictive legislation. Moreover, the Chinese population was decreasing because

there was a very short supply of women. The problem of
Japanese immigrants, however, remained. The government of
British Columbia reacted by denying such rights as voting and
entering into such professional fields as medicine and law to
those of Japanese descent, even if they were born in Canada
and had been educated in Canadian schools. Workers of
Japanese origin were not even allowed on public works
(Woodsworth, 1937). At the constant insistence of British
Columbia, Prime Minister King further negotiated with his
Japanese counterpart to impose more restrictions on Japanese
immigration to Canada. As a response, the Japanese government
informed the Dominion on August 22, 1923, that "the Japanese
do not, under the administrative measures now adopted, contem-
plate that the number of Japanese immigrants going to Canada
as household servants and agricultural labourers will exceed
one hundred fifty annually." (Cheng, 1931:136)

The cooperative effort between the governments of Canada
and Japan to restrict Japanese immigration to Canada lasted
until World War II with few anti-Japanese activities in
British Columbia. In anticipating a possible war, a committee
of senior civil servants considered the position of the
Japanese immigrants, should Japan become belligerent
(Sunahara, 1980). In February 1939 the committee concluded as
follows:

> [I]f the enemy should be an Asiatic
> power,...[i]t might become necessary in that
> contingency, to recommend the internment of
> nearly all enemy nationals, since it is
> recognized that public feeling in that section
> of Canada [British Columbia] on the part of
> Canadian citizens and other Asiatics might
> render this course necessary, not alone to
> avoid the danger of espionage and sabotage, but
> also for the protection of the person and
> property of enemy aliens. (Sunahara, 1980:100)

Following the recommendations of the committee and the out-
break of the Pacific War on December 7, 1941, the Royal
Canadian Navy began the impoundment of Japanese Canadian
fishing vessels. In addition, the Japanese language schools
were closed, the minority press was suppressed, and Japanese
persons were ordered to register with the R.C.M.P. (Sunahara,
1980).

After war was declared on the morning of February 24,
1942, the Canadian cabinet passed an order-in-council to grant
the power to the minister of justice to designate areas from
which "any and all persons" can be removed and detained. All
the Japanese were evacuated from the protected area on the
Pacific Coast, and provisions were made elsewhere (Sunahara,
1980). It is hard to believe that on February 20, 1942, the
Canadian government successively expanded its Japanese
Canadian policies, but, in matter of five days, "the Japanese

minority had changed, in the opinion of the Cabinet, from a 'problem' in need of protection from rioters to a threat to the safety of Pacific Coast defences as charged by the anti-Asian lobby of B.C." (Sunahara, 1980:112).

East Indian Immigrants

A review of the historical literature on the East Indians in Canada shows that until 1913 nothing other than a few newspaper reports had been written. Sihra (1913) published an article in an Indian journal in which it was stated that migration to Canada from the Indian subcontinent did not start until after the turn of the century. Jain (1971) stated that there were 45 East Indians in British Columbia in 1904-1905. However, Raj (1980) disproves Sihra's contention and argues that the earliest East Indian immigrants to Canada arrived in the year 1899. Some of these earlier immigrants landed in Victoria, others in Vancouver. Raj also quotes a figure of 258 East Indians in British Columbia during 1904, rather than the 45 mentioned by Jain. Jain provides some detail on the number of East Indians immigrating to Canada during the period 1904-1966, and his data are reproduced in Table 2.2.

From this table it is clear that the number of 45 East Indians in 1904-1905 increased to 387 in the year 1905-1906, 2,124 in 1906-1907 and 2,623 in 1907-1908. Almost all of these immigrants were Sikhs from Punjab, a northern state of India. It would seem that this selectivity was related to the fact that Sikh soldiers from the State of Punjab attended Queen Victoria's Jubilee in 1887, and they visited Canada on their way home. This visit made a lasting impression on the Sikhs resulting in the beginning of emigration from India to Canada (Story, 1967). Realizing the economic opportunities in Canada, as many as 5,000 Sikhs had arrived in British Columbia by 1908. This heavy emigration from India was partly due to a program of propaganda in northern India by some Canadian companies to stimulate interest in emigration (Muthanna, 1975). These early settlers found employment in the lumber industry, railway construction, and on farms (Williams, 1907). Unfortunately, this employment did not last for a long period of time, and, by the end of 1907, about 1,500 East Indians found themselves jobless. By this time, a hostile atmosphere had been created toward these immigrants by the local people. This atmosphere well described by Raj (1980) by quoting the press articles of that time:

> The press described the East Indian arrival as "Hindu Invasion." Frequently, it featured front page articles under captions such as "Invasion Threatened", "Hordes of Hungry Hindus Invade Vancouver City", "Agent of Hindus is...: Spying out of the Land", "The Invasion of British Columbia", "Hordes of Hindus on Steamer

Tartar", "Hindus Coming in Hundreds", "More are
on the Way", "Many Thousands More will Come",
and "Hindus are Expected to Fight to Enter
Canada". The press also portrayed the East
Indian immigrants in the worst possible light.
Captions such as "Hindus . . . Evade the
Police", "Fiendish Crime Done by Hindus",
"Hindus hold up Lonely Homes . . . Create a
Region of Terror in Suburbs", "Masked Hindu
Sandbags Vancouver woman", "Hindus Revel in
Litigation", "Hindu Quarters in Deplorable
State . . . with Filth and Alive with Rats",
"Get Rid of Hindus at Whatever Cost" and
similar headlines were quite common. (p. 67)

TABLE 2.2
East Indian Immigrants to Canada 1904 to 1971

Year	Immigrants	Year	Immigrants	Year	Immigrants
1904-05	45	1927	56	1949	54
1905-06	387	1928	52	1950	93
1906-07	2,124	1929	58	1951	99
1907-08	2,623	1930	80	1952	172
1908-09	6	1931	47	1953	140
1909-10	10	1932	62	1954	177
1910-11	5	1933	33	1955	249
1911-12	3	1934	33	1956	332
1913	5	1935	21	1957	334
1914	88	1936	13	1958	459
1915	Nil	1937	14	1959	741
1916	1	1938	14	1960	691
1917	Nil	1939	11	1961	744
1918	Nil	1940	6	1962	830
1919	Nil	1941	3	1963	1,331
1920	10	1942	Nil	1964	2,077
1921	13	1943	Nil	1965	3,491
1922	21	1944	Nil	1966	4,094
1923	40	1945	1	1967*	5,972
1924	46	1946	8	1968*	4,809
1925	62	1947	167	1969*	7,264
1926	60	1948	64	1970*	7,660
				1971*	7,049

Source: Sushil Jain (1971), East Indians in Canada, Supplement 9,
June, 1971, pp. 3, 8-9. The Hague: Research Group for European
Migration Problems.

*Figures refer to the Country of Citizenship and are taken from
Quarterly Immigration Bulletin, Department of Citizenship and
Immigration, Ottawa.

During this time the local politicians joined the local labour groups in denouncing the East Indian immigrants as a burden to the city and as destructive to the British way of life.

The federal government responded to the British Columbian people's concerns, and an order-in-council was issued in 1913 to stop further immigration from India. The order-in-council states:

> the Governor-General in Council may . . . prohibit the landing . . . of any immigrants who have come to Canada otherwise than by continuous journey from the country of which they are natives. (Raj, 1980:68)

As a result of this order-in-council, a most unfortunate incident for East Indian immigrants took place during 1914 (Morse, 1936). On May 23, 1914, about 376 East Indians arrived off Vancouver Harbour on a Japanese steamer, the Komagata Maru. They were all prohibited from landing except for a few who were able to prove that they were returning to Canada. The rest of them had to stay on the steamer off the coast of Vancouver while their cases were being examined in the British Columbia courts. After many days of waiting and much anxiety among the would-be immigrants, they were refused landing because they did not possess in their own right $200; they did not travel by continuous journey from their native country and they were not skilled labourers (Morse, 1936). About 175 local police and immigration officers, whose intentions were to place the passengers on board the Empress of India for a voyage to Hong Kong, were fought off by pieces of coal, wood, brick, and steel hurled from the decks of the Komagata Maru. Only after local East Indians were assured of compensation for legal expenses incurred in defending the victims of the Komagata Maru affair, was the ship allowed to sail. Later on, as British subjects entitled to family reconstitution, the Sikhs in Canada protested and felt that they had been denied the right to bring their relatives. In addition, there was further violence in India, and the case of the Komagata Maru became a cause celebre. Finally, as an outcome of the Imperial Conference of 1917, the East Indians were permitted to bring their wives and children to Canada. For the period from 1920 to 1923, those who came as dependents are presented below (Morse, 1936)

Year	Wives	Children
1920	-	-
1921	2	1
1922	4	4
1923	5	4

The Komagata Maru incident was a major factor in curtail-
ing immigration after 1914. Jain (1971) found that only 422
East Indians came to Canada between 1920 and 1930, and 338
came between 1930 and 1942. Even those who were already in
Canada faced many difficulties; for example, they were neither
allowed to vote in British Columbia nor permitted to practice
certain professions.
    Raj (1980) advances many reasons for excluding East
Indians from immigration. The dominant society alleged the
East Indians to be unassimilable. Raj (1980) makes these
reasons clear in a passage he quoted from an editorial in
The Colonist (September 13, 1907)

    [T]he people of the western races . . . of this
    broad and fair land . . . hope that civilization in
    the best and truest sense may advance and develop
    (sic) to a fuller degree than has yet been achieved.
    But the invitation or admission of these people, the
    Hindus, would threaten and even make impossible the
    realization of these people. . . . To prepare
    ourselves for the irrepressible conflict, Canada
    must be and remain a White Man's country. On this
    western frontier of the coming struggle. . . .
    Therefore we ought to maintain this country for the
    Anglo-Saxon and those races which are able to
    assimilate themselves to them. If this is done, we
    believe that history will repeat itself and the
    supremacy of our race will continue. We believe
    that Canada holds in its hand to a large degree the
    future of Caucasian civilization. (p. 69)

    When the political rights of the East Indian immigrants
were denied, as well as entry into professions such as
education, law, and pharmacy, this served as a poignant
reminder to the succeeding generations of their second-class
status (Morse, 1935). Demands for political quality increased
among the second and succeeding generations. Though not
openly, these immigrants were able to secure support of some
British Columbian politicians and academicians, most notably

that of Professor H. F. Angus. It was during the early 1940s, when the international climate was changing, that the East Indian community, with the support of the (CCF), was able to change the legislation of British Columbia and gain the municipal franchise (Norris, 1948).

2.2 POST-WORLD WAR II PERIOD

With the end of the war, the situation for immigration was different. It was felt that a larger population made sense from an economic point of view. There was also international pressure for increasing immigration (Timlin, 1957). Canada also wanted to play a larger role in international affairs. As a first step in this direction, Canada named its first full-time secretary of state for external affairs. Since Canada was concerned not to offend international opinion (Hawkins, 1972), it was necessary to change her immigration policies. The pre-World War II racial discriminatory policies were buried, and, in a publication for the Canadian Institute of International Affairs, a public servant noted that "racial discrimination was in disfavour in the international community but that it was easier to defend discrimination on an economic, political, or social basis, which served the same purpose since racial differences he noted, largely coincided with economic differences." (Beaujot and McQuillan, 1982:96) This was the basis for the post war immigration policies of Canada.

Unlike in the past, the post-war immigration policies were more universal in nature, and, hence, it does not make sense to discuss the Chinese, Japanese and East Indians separately. In the following paragraphs, we will outline briefly the evolution of the government policies on immigration during the post-war period. Later on, we will present how these policies affected Asian immigrants in particular.

In 1947 the Liberal government prepared a formal immigration policy, and orders-in-council were passed. The policy was meant to encourage immigrants from Europe. Although the policy did not explicitly deal with the omission of non-white immigrants, the government manipulations implied that non-white immigrants were excluded de facto. When the Department of Citizenship and Immigration was created in 1949, the immigration officers were given further discretionary powers in evaluating immigrants. The most favoured groups were the British, New Zealanders, Australians, South Africans, Irish, Americans, and French. The only orientals admitted to Canada were the wives and unmarried children, under eighteen years of age, of Canadian citizens. However, as a gesture to Commonwealth relations, special arrangements were made for immigration from India, Pakistan, and Ceylon in 1951. According to these arrangements, the Canadian government agreed to admit 150 Indians, 100 Pakistanis, and 50 Ceylonese every year.

A revised immigration policy was introduced in the House of Commons in 1952, which became the Immigration Act of 1953 and granted extensive discretionary powers to the minister of citizenship and immigration. The new act clearly prohibited immigrants of Asian origin, stating that persons with peculiar customs, habits, modes of life, or methods of holding property could be refused entry into Canada. Asians were further excluded for the reasons that they could not be readily integrated and assimilated in Canadian national life and were likely to experience problems in dealing with extreme climatic conditions. The minister could intepret these clauses in various ways, because of his discretionary power, to exclude non-white immigrants and encourage whites. In 1957, new immigration quotas were fixed for the Indian subcontinent of 300 Indians, 100 Pakistanis, and 50 Ceylonese per year (Rawlyk, 1962). In practice, these numbers were rarely achieved due to the lack of facilities processing applications, and in 1962 the agreement was terminated (Richmond and Kalbach, 1980).

The Liberal government was defeated by the Conservatives in 1957, and important modifications took place in the immigration policy. The first female cabinet minister, Mrs. Ellen Fairclough, issued new immigration regulations. This new policy stressed education, training, and skills as the main considerations of admissibility, regardless of the country of emigration (Rawlyk, 1962). The minister further made an important qualification of the so-called "non-racial" regulations. Governmental regulations, which limited the annual number of immigrants from the Indian subcontinent, remained in force until a new quota agreement was reached. Had there been no restriction on the number of immigrants, many qualified immigrants from the subcontinent would have taken the opportunity to migrate to Canada.

A new immigration policy was brought in by the Liberal government on October 1, 1967. This was intended to abolish discrimination and serve the manpower needs of the Canadian economy. The new policy identified three categories of immigrants--sponsored, nominated, and independent (Kage, 1967). The sponsored immigrants could originate in any country. A Canadian citizen or permanent resident of Canada was entitled to sponsor his immediate dependents such as spouse, parents or grandparents, and dependent children below the age of twenty-one. Nominated immigrants included unmarried children of twenty-one years or over, or a married son or daughter under twenty-one years of age. It also covered a brother or sister, a nephew, niece, uncle, aunt, or grandchild. An independent migrant was one who qualified on his or her own merits: education, skill, age, personal qualities, employment arrangements, knowledge of English and/or French, and place of destination. A point system was used to assess independent and nominated persons. The assessment system provided 100 assessment units which were distributed according to the characteristics of a given applicant. Twenty units were given for the applicant's education or occupational training, 15 units for personal qualities, 15 units for the applicant's occupation in Canada, 10 units for his or her professional status, 10 units for an age under thirty-five, 10 units for an arranged job in Canada, 10 units for fluency in English and French, 5 units for a relative in Canada, and 5 units for readiness to go wherever job opportunities were available in Canada (Kage, 1967). This mixture of objective and subjective assessments still gave an immigration officer a decisive role regarding who entered Canada, but it did open the door to Asian immigration. In the span of four years, beginning in 1967, the proportion of Asian immigrants in Canada almost doubled. The proportion of immigrants of Asian origin was less than 2 percent until 1961; it rose to 6.7 percent by 1966; and for the period from 1967 to 1971 it increased to 13.6 percent (Richmond and Kalbach, 1980:65)

Asian Immigrants

At the end of World War II, there were about 23,000 Japanese, 35,500 Chinese, and 6,000 East Indian immigrants in Canada. After the war, conditions improved for Japanese immigrants in particular and Asian immigrants in general. However, improved conditions and change in the Immigration Act of 1967 did not motivate Japanese to migrate to Canada; perhaps there were fewer "push" factors at home, or the recent history of Canadian abuse discouraged Japanese immigrants. In fact, soon after the war, as many as 4,000 Japanese, including some who had obtained Canadian citizenship as a result of the Canadian citizenship Act of 1947, went back to Japan (The Canadian Family Tree, 1979:139)

During World War II, many Chinese-Canadians served in the defence forces and were generally loyal to their country of residence. Fortunately for the Chinese, the end of war brought good news, including repeal of the Chinese Immigration Act, and Canadian citizens of Chinese origin were granted the full rights of citizenship. (The Canadian Family Tree, 1979) This changed the whole character of Chinese life in Canada. Most of the eligible Chinese immigrants became naturalized citizens and were able to bring their families and relatives to Canada. Between 1946 and 1965, about 36,370 Chinese entered Canada as family members of Chinese-Canadians. Especially after the Immigration Act of 1967, Chinese immigration increased in tempo, and a total of 47,759 Chinese arrived between 1963 and 1970. (The Canadian Family Tree, 1979:45)

The post-war history of East Indian immigrants is similar to that of the Chinese. The East Indians also enjoyed the benefits of the Canadian Citizenship Act of 1947 as well as British Columbia's enactment of franchise regulations granting them the right to vote (Encyclopedia Canadiana, 1970). Like the Chinese group, the volume and composition of the East Indian immigrants to Canada was changed after the point system came into effect in 1967. In 1967 alone, 5,924 East Indians entered Canada. Unlike earlier immigrants to Canada, they were highly qualified professionals (The Canadian Family Tree, 1979:113). They also came from different parts of their native country as evidenced by their linguistic and religious heterogeneity. After 1967, persons of Indian origin not only came directly from India, but also from other parts of the world, such as Fiji, East Africa, Trinidad and Tobago, Guyana, South Africa, and the United Kingdom. (The Canadian Family Tree, 1979)

Record of Asians by Census Dates

Table 2.3 summarizes the account of Asians in Canada by census dates. Canadian census authorities published figures for only Chinese and Japanese perhaps because historically these have been the only two dominant groups from Asia. The figures for the East Indians have been derived from Table 2.2; these figures are only estimates as we do not have actual census figures. The fluctuations in figures for Chinese and Japanese are consistent with historical discussions. There was a steady increase for both groups until the beginning of World War II when a sudden drop occurred. The immigrant flow from Asia did not show an upward trend again until the 1952 act was modified in 1962. The new regulations technically eliminated discrimination on the basis of race or nationality. The new set of criertia employed for independent immigrants were based on education, occupation, and technical skills, against which applicants would have to score 50 out of a possible 100 points in order to be admitted. This resulted in an unprecedented increase in immigration from Asia. The pace of immigration was further accelerated when the point system was revised in 1967 to make a provision for visitors to apply for landed immigrant status while in Canada. An all-time high was reached during 1967 and 1971. Nearly 119,000 Chinese and more than 37,000 Japanese were counted in the 1971 census. The figures for the East Indians show a uniform increase until 1951 and an exponential increase thereafter. In 1971, there were as many as 61,535 East Indians in Canada. The figures for the 1981 census are even more dramatic especially for Chinese and East Indians. Table 2.3 shows that from 1971 to 1981 the Chinese population in Canada increased by 243 percent and the East Indian population by 290 percent.

Though there has been an unprecedented increase in the total number of Asian immigrants to Canada in recent years, Indra (1980) argues that the selection of immigrants from Asia was not purely based on individual skills and abilities, and Asia is not well represented with reference to her potential immigrant population in the Canadian immigration picture. This is partly due to a lack of immigration centres in Asia.

TABLE 2.3

Distribution of Asian Ethnic Groups By Census Dates, 1871 to 1981

Census Dates

Ethnicity	1871	1881	1901	1911	1921	1931	1941	1951	1961	1971	1981[a]
Chinese*	-	4,383	17,312	27,831	39,587	46,519	34,627	32,528	58,197	118,815	289,245
Japanese*	-	-	4,738	9,067	15,868	23,342	23,149	21,663	29,157	37,260	40,995
East Indians**	-	-	-	5,200	5,320	5,842	6,052	6,538	10,577	67,930	196,390
Other	4	-	1,681	1,115	5,139	8,845	10,236	12,098	23,822	61,535	76,845
Total*	4	4,383	23,731	43,213	65,914	84,548	74,064	72,827	121,753	285,540	603,475

* Figures for these groups have been taken from K. G. Basavarajappa and Bali Ram (1983); "Population and Migration", pp. A154-184 in F. H. Leacy (eds.), Historical Statistics of Canada (Second Edition), Ottawa: Statistics Canada.

** Figures for this group are estimated from Table 2.2 without accounting for mortality and emigration.

a Figures for 1981 census are taken from 1981 Census of Canada Catalogue 92-911 (vol. 1 - National Series):1-7 to 1-12.

Before 1975, there were only four immigration centres in Asia, all located in the capitals (Tokyo, New Delhi, Hong Kong, and Manila) of what were then Canada's first, second, fourth, and fifth Asian trading partners, respectively (Indra, 1980). This compares unfavourably to the distribution of Canadian immigration centres in other countries. For example, there were seven centres in the United Kingdom alone. According to 1975 figures, out of the sixty immigration centres, forty-six were in cities which had Canadian trade centres in 1966 (Indra, 1980). Indra has shown that there is a direct relationship between the Canadian trade centres of 1966 and the present-day immigration centres. If the recent immigration from Asia has increased, it is because Canadian trade with Asia has also increased. The Canadian government is playing a key role in promoting Asian markets for Canadian business. Canada seems to have identified the newly emerging Asian nations as being of future significance to Canadian trade (Indra, 1980). There are also other factors as well, political and bureaucratic, which make Asian immigration to Canada more difficult. It may be true that Canadian immigration regulations are intended to decide about immigrants based purely on individual traits, but the reality is still far from the intention. This can most easily be seen in the lack of immigration centres in Asia.

After the point system was introduced in immigration regulations, the composition of the immigrant population to Canada changed. A shift toward a continuous increase of non-white immigration, especially from Asia, has been noticed (Anderson and Frideres, 1980). Since the analysis for this study will be based on 1971 census data, it may be useful to examine the age-sex composition of Asian ethnic groups, which was obtained from Statistics Canada.

Tables 2.4 and 2.5, which are based on unpublished 1971 data obtained from Statistics Canada, give an idea of the sex composition, age composition, and rural-urban distribution of the Asian population in Canda. The urban residents have been further classified into three separate categories: those living in cities of more than 500,000 inhabitants, those living in places with a population of more than 100,000 but less than 500,000, and those living in urban areas of less than 100,000.

Table 2.4 shows the broad patterns of age and sex composition for the Asian ethnic groups. The broader age categories indicate that more than 60 percent of East Indians are concentrated in the 15-44 age group, followed by nearly 50 percent of the Chinese and around 47 percent of the Japanese. In the age group 45-64, nearly 19 percent of the Japanese, 12 percent of the Chinese, and only 6 percent of the East Indians are found. This vividly indicates that the East Indian population in Canada belongs to a relatively younger age structure, the Japanese constitute the older age structure, and the Chinese are intermediate.

TABLE 2.4
Percentage Distribution of Asian Ethnic Groups by Age Groups and Sex, Canada, 1971

Males

Age Groups	Chinese Numbers	%	Japanese Numbers	%	East Indian Numbers	%	Other Asian Numbers	%
15	18,930	30.14	4,895	25.80	10,335	29.16	9,035	27.47
15-44	31,420	50.03	8,880	46.90	22,545	63.61	17,715	53.85
45-64	6,630	10.56	3,700	19.54	2,135	6.03	4,870	14.80
65 +	5,825	9.28	1,475	7.79	420	1.19	1,285	3.91
Total	62,800	100.00	18,935	100.00	35,440	100.00	32,895	100.00

Females

Age Groups	Chinese Numbers	%	Japanese Numbers	%	East Indian Numbers	%	Other Asian Numbers	%
15	17,815	31.80	4,730	25.81	9,685	29.81	8,345	29.14
15-44	26,635	47.55	8,810	48.08	20,560	63.28	13,805	48.20
45-64	8,040	14.35	3,375	18.42	1,720	5.29	4,670	16.31
65 +	3,520	6.28	1,405	7.67	530	1.63	1,825	6.37
Total	56,015	100.00	18,325	100.00	32,490	100.00	28,640	100.00

Source: Unpublished 1971 census data of Canada.

TABLE 2.5

Percentage Distribution of Asian Ethnic Groups by Type of Residence, 1971

Type of Residence	Ethnicity							
	Chinese		Japanese		East Indian		Other Asian	
	Numbers	%	Numbers	%	Numbers	%	Numbers	%
Rural	3,315	2.79	4,170	11.19	3,970	5.84	2,760	4.49
Urban	115,500	97.21	33,085	88.79	63,950	94.14	58,770	95.51
500,000 +	77,215	64.98	22,815	61.23	40,060	58.97	36,935	60.02
100,000 - 499,999	20,515	17.27	4,095	10.99	10,790	15.88	11,345	18.44
less than 100,000	17,770	14.96	6,175	16.57	13,100	19.28	10,490	17.05
Total	118,820	100.00	37,260	100.00	67,930	100.00	61,535	100.00

Source: Unpublished 1971 census data of Canada.

A closer comparison of the three ethnic groups in terms of their sex composition proves interesting. In the case of the Chinese, there are 62,800 males and 56,015 females (sex ratio of 112 males per 100 females); in the case of the Japanese, there are 18,935 males and 18,325 females (sex ratio of 103 males per 100 females); and among the East Indians, there are 35,440 males and 32,490 females (sex ratio of 109 males per 100 females). The sex differences among the ethnic groups are small, yet of interest. The higher sex ratio in favour of males among Chinese is true historically. As we have indicated, most of the Chinese immigrants were single young men before World War II. Moreover, the Chinese did not dream of permanent emigration because of their traditionally strong tie with their families, and only adult males emigrated to Canada for economic opportunities (Lai, 1980). This reasoning is often true for the East Indians as well.

Table 2.5 presents the distribution of Asian ethnic groups by type of residence. The proportional representation of the four groups is quite similar with little variation. More than 11 percent of the Japanese reside in rural areas followed by nearly 6 percent of the East Indians and less than 3 percent of the Chinese. All three groups are concentrated in large urban areas with a population of more than 500,000, perhaps because most of them are highly educated technical and professional people. (The Canadian Family Tree, 1979:46) Their education and technical skills make it possible for them to find jobs in the urban areas. The people who have settled in rural areas are probably those who came to Canada before the new law came into effect in 1967. It is possible that these were the early settlers from Asia who were mostly farmers and workers in the forest industry.

2.3 SOCIO-ECONOMIC CHARACTERISTICS

Type of Residence by Marital Status

Using 1971 Census data, Balakrishnan et al. (1979) have demonstrated that fertility levels vary by province as well as by level of urbanization. They also found that the variations between rural and urban areas are more significant than the differences among the provinces. The urban fertility rates are about 75 percent of the level of the rural fertility rate. (Balakrishnan et al., 1979:50) Hence, it is worthwhile to look at the distribution of Asian married women by place of residence in Canada.

It is clear from Table 2.5 that nearly 90 percent of the Asian ethnic groups, regardless of their marital status or geographical origins, are residing in the urban areas. This is perhaps because the immigrants are selected on a point system, which makes it easier for urbanites to gain admission. They settle in Canadian urban areas in continuation of their residential pattern at their origin though they are encouraged to settle in areas of high labour demand. Indra (1980) also argues that most Asian immigrants who have been selected have been affected by industrialization and by Western ideas and practices. These types of people in Asian countries live in urban industrialized contexts.

Table 2.6 reveals the marital status of Asian ethnic groups by type of residence and sex. More than 40 percent of males and females are married in almost all ethnic groups regardless of their place of residence; the rest are mostly single people. The interesting feature of this table is that the percentage of singles is higher in rural areas for all the ethnic groups and for both the sexes. However, the differences are not very significant when compared to their urban counterparts. The only notable difference among categories in this table is the higher incidence of "other" marital status (widowed, divorced, and separated) among females across all other variables. Among other factors, this may be due to a higher percentage of widows among females, resulting from earlier mortality of males.

Nativity and Type of Residence

Balakrishnan et al. (1979) found in their study that foreign-born women have much lower fertility than native-born women and that fertility differences by nativity are greater for younger cohorts. They argue that this is because immigrants have been selected on education and other socio-economic and demographic variables. Since nativity is related to fertility, it may be useful to know the distribution of Asian groups by nativity and type of residence.

Table 2.7a has been included to show Asian immigrants by nativity and type of residence. As one would expect, the foreign-born have settled mainly in urban areas where employment opportunities are more varied and plentiful and they are more competent with the adjustment problems of urban areas as they have been mostly selected based on their education and technical skills. People with higher education and occupational skills in Asian countries are usually found in urban and industrial sectors.

The pattern of native-born Asian origin groups is also as one would expect: The proportion of rural residents is higher among the native-born Asian ethnic groups compared to the foreign-born Asian populations. The reasons could be that a higher proportion of the earlier immigrants from the Asian countries, who came to work either in mines or railroad construction, must have settled in rural areas and continue to live there. It is interesting to note that among native-born persons, the Japanese have the highest percentage of rural dwellers and the Chinese are the most urbanized.

Table 2.7b displays the percentage of native born by each ethnic group. More than 75 percent of the Japanese are native born compared to 37 percent of the Chinese and only 20 percent

TABLE 2.6

Percentage Distributions of Asian Ethnic Groups by Marital Status and Sex, 1971

Ethnic Groups	Type of Residence	Males				Females			
		Marital Status				Marital Status			
		Single	Married	Others	Total	Single	Married	Others	Total
Chinese	Rural	58.9	37.1	4.0	100.0	50.0	43.0	7.0	100.0
	Urban	54.9	47.1	4.0	100.0	48.5	42.4	9.1	100.0
	Total	55.0	41.0	4.0	100.0	48.6	42.4	9.0	100.0
Japanese	Rural	56.8	39.9	3.3	100.0	47.6	45.5	6.9	100.0
	Urban	50.3	46.4	3.3	100.0	44.0	47.0	9.0	100.0
	Total	51.1	45.7	3.2	100.0	44.4	46.8	8.8	100.0
East Indian	Rural	57.1	40.9	2.0	100.0	53.1	42.2	4.5	100.0
	Urban	53.3	44.7	2.0	100.0	53.6	42.3	4.1	100.0
	Total	53.5	44.5	2.0	100.0	53.6	42.3	4.1	100.0
Other Asian	Rural	56.1	41.0	2.9	100.0	53.9	40.9	6.1	100.0
	Urban	53.3	43.7	3.0	100.0	47.6	41.5	10.9	100.0
	Total	53.5	43.5	3.0	100.0	47.9	41.5	10.6	100.0

Source: Unpublished 1971 census data of Canada.

TABLE 2.7A

Percentage Distribution of Asian Ethnic Groups in Canada by Nativity and Type of Residence, 1971

Ethnic Group	Native Born			Foreign Born			Total		
	Rural	Urban	Total	Rural	Urban	Total	Rural	Urban	Total
Chinese	(3.6)19.5	(96.4)40.9	(100.0)39.3	(2.3)28.5	(97.7)43.6	(100.0)43.1	(2.8)23.3	(97.2)42.6	(100.0)41.6
Japanese	(11.6)39.9	(88.4)24.1	(100.0)25.2	(9.9)15.2	(90.1) 4.9	(100.0) 5.3	(11.2)29.3	(88.8)12.2	(100.0)13.0
East Indian	(9.3)15.5	(90.7)12.0	(100.0)12.2	(5.0)44.6	(95.0)30.7	(100.0)31.1	(5.8)27.9	(94.2)23.6	(100.0)23.8
Other Asian	(8.0)25.1	(92.7)23.1	(100.0)23.2	(2.0)11.7	(98.0)20.8	(100.0)20.5	(4.5)19.4	(95.5)21.7	(100.0)21.6
Total	(7.3)100.0	(92.7)100.0	(100.0)100.0	(3.5)100.0	(96.5)100.0	(100.0)100.0	(5.0)100.0	(95.0)100.0	(100.0)100.0

NOTE: Figures in the parentheses indicate row percentages.

TABLE 2.7B

Percentage Distribution of Native Born by Residence and Ethnicity, 1971

Type of Residence	Ethnicity				
	Chinese	Japanese	East Indian	Other Asian	Total
Rural	48.0	77.9	31.9	74.3	57.3
Urban	36.4	74.8	19.2	40.4	37.9
Total	36.7	75.1	20.0	41.9	38.85

Source: Unpublished 1971 Census Data of Canada

where:

Xi is the total wealth in each income category
Yi is the total family heads in ith income category and
n is the the number of income categories.

The results shown in Table 2.8 reveals that among immigrants the Chinese and Japanese generally have higher levels of inequality in the distribution of income compared to the East Indians. This pattern remains the same even when the duration of stay in Canada is considered, except for the periods 1951-1955 and 1966-1971. The higher ratios for the Chinese compared to the other two groups indicate in-group variations in socio-economic achievement. The lower ratios among the Indians imply a more equitable distribution of wealth.

It would have been interesting to compare the income disparity between the immigrants and their native-born counterparts. We could have gained further insight regarding the structural assimilative process of the immigrants, and we also could have assessed the income inequality between the two groups. Unfortunately, we did not have the family income breakdown by place of birth.

Labour Force and Occupational Divisions

It is clear that a woman's occupational position is related to her childbearing. Those who work mainly in traditional occupations, such as agriculture, handicrafts, or domestic service, have fertility levels very similar to non-working women (Ahdab-Yehia, 1977:173). However, those who participate in more modern occupations, such as secretaries, bank tellers, and supermarket clerks, may develop the modern working-women life-styles associated with small family size norms. Birdsall (1976) argues that simple labour force participation by women does not affect fertility, unless this status involves a real extension of roles beyond the family and into the economic and political realm. Hence, it is useful to look at the pattern of labour force participation among Asian males and females.

Table 2.9 presents the Asian ethnic labour force, fifteen years of age and over, by major occupational division and by sex. A closer look at the table reveals that, in the professional and managerial categories for all immigrant groups, males are over-represented. On the other hand, in the clerical, medical, and health categories, females outnumber the males. Moreover, nearly forty percent of the teaching category is occupied by women in immigrant groups except for the Japanese. In the case of the Japanese, this proportion is in favour of males. The Chinese women seem to be quite active in religious activities.

There are some distinct differences in Asian ethnic occupational concentrations. The Chinese males have their main occupational concentration in the services category with 36.3 percent; the second preference is given to sales with 10.2 percent; and the third preference is for the natural sciences with 8.6 percent. The occupational preference of the Japanese women is different from those of the Chinese women. Though Japanese women's second largest category is service, the representation in the service sector employment by these women is only 12.5 percent in comparison with the clerical sector which is more than 32 percent. Japanese men do not seem to have a strong preference for any one kind of job. Farming, sales, and sciences are all equally important for them. This goes back to the reasoning that recent immigrants from Japan are concentrated in sales and science, but those who came earlier settled in rural areas and preferred their occupation to be farming.

The case of East Indians is different, with respect to their occupational preference, from the Chinese and Japanese. This is perhaps because the East Indians mostly migrated to Canada after the point system was introduced. Hence, they are selected to some extent by their education and occupational skills. Primarily because of this, the highest concentration for males is in the natural sciences category, with 14.8 percent. For females it is medicine and health, with 32.7 percent. The high concentration of females in this category may reflect the fact that the female immigrants from India during recent years are mostly doctors, paramedical workers, and nurses. It is particularly true that a number of few nurses come from the southern state of India, Kerala, where the literacy rate is the highest in India, for both men and women. There is also a large Christian population in Kerala, and they may have found it easier to migrate to a Christian country like Canada. Like the Chinese and Japanese women, there is a high concentration of East Indian females in the clerical category, the teaching profession, and the service sector. East Indian males are in medicine and health and in primary sector occupations such as processing as well. The immigrants in the processing sector are probably those who came to Canada before 1951.

Education by Sex

The inverse relationship between education and fertility can be observed in almost all societies--the more educated have smaller families (Freedman et al., 1959; Whelpton et al., 1966; Westoff and Ryder, 1971 and 1977; Henripin, 1972; Balakrishnan et al., 1979). Westoff and Ryder (1971) argue that the more educated have smaller families because schooling brings a rational outlook to one's life and affects labour force participation and attitudes toward children, sex roles, religious beliefs, and effective use of contraception. In

Table 2.9

Percentage Distribution of Asian Labour Force 15 Years and Over
by Major Occupational Divisions and Sex, Canada, 1971

Occupation	Chinese			Japanese		
	Males	Females	Total	Males	Females	Total
Managerial	82.6(2.5)	17.4(0.8)	100.0(1.8)	83.6(4.1)	16.4(1.3)	100.0(3.1)
Natural Sciences	88.7(8.6)	11.3(1.7)	100.0(5.9)	91.7(9.0)	8.3(1.3)	100.0(6.0)
Social Sciences	48.1(0.6)	51.9(1.0)	100.0(0.7)	44.4(0.6)	55.6(1.3)	100.0(0.9)
Religion	55.6(0.1)	44.4(0.1)	100.0(0.1)	85.7(0.2)	14.3(0.1)	100.0(0.2)
Teaching	57.9(2.5)	42.1(2.9)	100.0(2.7)	44.9(3.0)	55.1(6.0)	100.0(4.2)
Medicine & Health	45.5(3.6)	54.5(6.8)	100.0(4.8)	33.3(2.1)	66.7(6.8)	100.0(3.9)
Artistic	77.1(0.9)	22.9(0.4)	100.0(0.7)	69.2(1.5)	30.8(1.0)	100.0(1.3)
Clerical	30.8(6.6)	69.2(23.2)	100.0(13.0)	25.5(7.0)	74.5(32.9)	100.0(16.9)
Sales	69.2(10.2)	30.8(7.2)	100.0(9.1)	66.8(9.3)	33.2(7.5)	100.0(8.6)
Services	71.2(36.3)	28.8(23.1)	100.0(31.2)	49.2(7.5)	50.8(12.5)	100.0(9.4)
Farming	53.8(1.7)	46.2(2.3)	100.0(1.9)	79.5(9.4)	20.5(3.9)	100.0(7.3)
Other Primary	95.8(0.3)	4.2(0.0)	100.0(0.2)	98.4(5.1)	1.6(0.1)	100.0(3.2)
Processing	62.8(3.1)	37.1(2.9)	100.0(3.0)	61.5(4.3)	28.5(4.4)	100.0(4.4)
Machining	89.2(1.2)	10.8(0.2)	100.0(0.8)	96.6(3.4)	3.4(0.2)	100.0(2.2)
Construction	100.0(1.6)	-.-(-)	100.0(1.0)	98.9(7.3)	1.1(0.1)	100.0(4.5)
Transport Equip.	95.2(2.0)	4.8(0.2)	100.0(1.3)	96.4(2.2)	3.6(0.1)	100.0(1.4)
Other	51.4(18.2)	48.6(27.1)	100.0(32.6)	65.4(23.9)	34.6(20.4)	100.0(22.6)
Total	61.2(100.0)	38.8(100.0)	100.0(100.0)	61.7(100.0)	38.3(100.0)	100.0(100.0)

| | East Indian | | | Other Asian | | |
Occupation	Males	Females	Total	Males	Females	Total
Managerial	84.5(4.2)	15.5(1.2)	100.0(3.0)	87.9(6.1)	12.1(1.6)	100.0(4.6)
Natural Sciences	92.8(14.8)	7.2(1.7)	100.0(9.6)	93.9(7.4)	6.1(0.9)	100.0(5.2)
Social Sciences	59.6(1.3)	40.4(1.3)	100.0(1.3)	62.7(1.0)	37.3(1.2)	100.0(1.1)
Religion	80.0(0.1)	20.0(0.0)	100.0(0.1)	87.5(0.2)	12.5(0.0)	100.0(0.1)
Teaching	60.2(8.4)	39.8(8.4)	100.0(8.4)	60.5(4.2)	39.5(5.4)	100.0(4.6)
Medicine & Health	28.1(8.5)	71.9(32.7)	100.0(18.2)	46.6(4.2)	53.4(9.5)	100.0(6.0)
Artistic	69.2(0.6)	30.8(0.4)	100.0(0.5)	72.5(1.6)	27.5(1.2)	100.0(1.4)
Clerical	36.3(9.2)	63.7(24.2)	100.0(15.2)	35.6(8.8)	64.4(31.0)	100.0(16.4)
Sales	76.2(5.6)	23.8(2.6)	100.0(4.4)	72.4(15.5)	27.6(11.5)	100.0(14.1)
Services	53.6(4.8)	46.4(6.3)	100.0(5.4)	63.2(9.6)	36.8(10.9)	100.0(10.0)
Farming	63.0(1.7)	37.0(1.5)	100.0(1.6)	74.7(1.3)	25.3(0.9)	100.0(1.2)
Other Primary	95.0(0.9)	5.0(0.1)	100.0(0.5)	93.1(0.6)	6.9(0.1)	100.0(0.5)
Processing	91.7(9.4)	8.3(1.3)	100.0(6.2)	77.8(2.9)	22.2(1.6)	100.0(2.4)
Machining	94.7(4.4)	5.3(0.4)	100.0(2.8)	95.3(4.9)	4.7(0.5)	100.0(3.4)
Construction	98.8(1.9)	1.2(0.0)	100.0(1.2)	99.4(4.2)	0.6(0.0)	100.0(2.8)
Transport Equip.	96.8(2.0)	3.2(0.1)	100.0(1.3)	98.0(2.3)	2.0(0.1)	100.0(1.6)
Other	65.2(22.3)	23.8(17.9)	100.0(20.5)	67.5(25.2)	32.5(25.2)	100.0(24.7)
Total	60.1(100.0)	39.9(100.0)	100.0(100.0)	66.1(100.0)	33.9(100.0)	100.0(100.0)

Note: Figures in the parentheses indicate column percentages.

Source: Unpublished 1971 Census Data of Canada.

Canada, Balakrishnan et al. (1979) found that, even after controlling for factors such as religion, labour force experience of women, or migration status, the inverse relationship between education and fertility still exists.

Table 2.10 displays the educational differences among the Asian ethnic groups. This table reveals that persons of East Indian origin in Canada are highly educated compared to their Chinese and Japanese counterparts. About 40 percent of the East Indian men and 30 percent of the women hold a university degree; the corresponding figures for the Chinese and Japanese migrants are below 16 percent. It is therefore no wonder that immigrants of Indian origin are engaged in such professional activities as science and medicine. In general, however, the modal category of educational attainment among Asians is the secondary level.

Religious Composition

Studies in both developing and developed countries have found fertility differentials among religious groups. Visaria (1974) and Rele and Kanitkar (1976) in India found significantly higher fertility for the Muslims than the Hindus. Based on his review of the fertility trends in several Muslim countries, Kirk (1967:154) came to the conclusion that "the uniformly high birth rate of Muslim communities is related to the influence of Islam." In the developed world, researchers such as Glass (1968), Burch (1966), Freedman et al. (1959), Whelpton et al. (1966), and Ryder and Westoff (1971) have found that Catholics have higher fertility rates than non-Catholics. Goldscheider (1971) hypothesized that the effects of religion on fertility behaviour and attitudes are due to the differences in church doctrine or religious ideology with respect to fertility control. In view of this, it is useful to examine the religious composition of Asian groups in Canada.

Table 2.11 shows the religious composition of Asian ethnic groups. Among the Chinese and the Japanese immigrants, regardless of type of residence, the major religious denomination is Christianity, with more than 50 percent belonging to this group. A large proportion (44 percent) of Chinese immigrants did not associate themselves with any religion. Among the Japanese, Buddhism was the second largest religious denomination, and those who do not associate with any religion is about 17 percent. According to the table, more than 54 percent of the East Indians belong to other religious categories, probably Sikhism, Hinduism, or Islam. Most of the early immigrants from northern India belong to Sikhism, and immigrants from Pakistan mostly belong to Islam; the rest are generally Hindus. The second largest category among East Indians are Christians with more than 41 percent. These are mostly recent immigrants from Kerala and the urban areas of India. Among the immigrants whose ethnicity is

Table 2.10

Percentage Distribution of Asian Population 15 Years and Over by
Education, Sex and Ethnicity, Canada, 1971

Level of Education

Ethnicity	Sex	Elementary	Secondary	Some University	University Degree	Total
Chinese	Males	26.2 (53.0)	45.6 (52.1)	12.3 (61.9)	15.9 (70.7)	100.0 (55.8)
	Females	29.2 (47.0)	52.9 (47.9)	9.6 (38.1)	8.3 (29.3)	100.0 (44.2)
	Total	27.5 (100.0)	48.8 (100.0)	11.1 (100.0)	12.5 (100.0)	100.0 (100.0)
Japanese	Males	18.3 (49.0)	57.1 (48.1)	10.1 (54.6)	14.5 (65.9)	100.0 (50.8)
	Females	19.7 (51.0)	63.9 (51.9)	8.7 (45.4)	7.7 (34.1)	100.0 (49.2)
	Total	19.0 (100.0)	60.4 (100.0)	9.4 (100.0)	11.2 (100.0)	100.0 (100.0)
East Indian	Males	8.8 (43.2)	35.5 (51.2)	16.3 (49.5)	39.4 (59.7)	100.0 (53.0)
	Females	13.0 (56.8)	38.2 (48.8)	18.7 (50.5)	30.1 (40.3)	100.0 (47.0)
	Total	10.0 (100.0)	36.8 (100.0)	17.4 (100.0)	35.0 (100.0)	100.0 (100.0)
Other Asian	Males	18.2 (47.0)	47.8 (50.8)	13.5 (62.5)	20.6 (74.3)	100.0 (55.0)
	Females	25.0 (53.0)	56.4 (49.2)	9.9 (37.5)	8.7 (25.7)	100.0 (45.0)
	Total	21.2 (100.0)	51.7 (100.0)	11.9 (100.0)	15.2 (100.0)	100.0 (100.0)

Note: Figures in the parentheses indicate column percentages.
Source: Unpublished 1971 Census Data of Canada

TABLE 2.11
Distribution of Asian Ethnic Groups by Religion, Canada, 1971

Religion	Chinese	Japanese	East Indian	Other Asian
Christian	50.8	53.3	41.1	74.0
Buddhist	1.9	27.7	0.4	0.7
Confucian	1.7	-	-	-
No Religion	44.1	17.3	3.8	4.6
Other	1.4	1.8	54.6	20.7
Total	100.0	100.0	100.0	100.0

Source: Unpublished 1971 census data of Canada.

classified as "other Asian," nearly 75 percent are Christian. It is possible that they are mostly from the Philippines, which is predominantly Roman Catholic.

Patterns in Language Spoken at Home

One of the hypotheses we intend to evaluate in the study of fertility differentials of Asians is the efficacy of their assimilation process into Canadian society. Richmond and Kalbach (1980) argue that language is one of the key traits that requires much attention in the study of assimilation or acculturation. Interaction and communication with the native born are necessary requisites for acculturation. As they put it, language is a vehicle for the transmission of culture and fluency; the native language will increase one's familiarity with that culture as a growing child or as a newly arrived immigrant. However, the extent of learning that can occur is a function of time and the possibility of change in immigrant behaviour.

Table 2.12 gives some indication of language patterns by broad age groups and ethnicity. A close examination of different ethnic groups by age reveals varying language patterns. For Chinese, in the youngest and oldest age groups, the percentage speaking their ethnic language is higher than the middle-age group, 25-34. The children of the 0-4 age group are usually at home and are most likely to communicate with their parents in their ethnic language unless the parents speak a langauge other than Chinese at home. Similarly, older people who came to Canada did not go to school here and, even

TABLE 2.12
Percentage Distribution of Asian Ethnic Groups by Age and
Language Spoken at Home, Canada, 1971

Ethnicity and Language	Age Groups			
	0-4	25-34	65+	Total
Chinese				
Chinese	65.3	63.2	83.8	62.4
Other	34.7	36.8	16.2	37.6
Japanese				
Japanese	23.6	27.2	77.7	24.5
Other	76.4	72.8	22.3	75.5
East Indians				
East Indian	28.3	28.8	32.1	29.4
Other	71.7	71.2	67.9	70.6
Other Asian				
English	50.0	41.6	31.8	48.9
French	9.6	11.7	11.5	11.9
Other	40.4	46.7	56.7	39.2

Source: Unpublished 1971 census data of Canada.

if they know English, it is only for the purposes of employment. However, relatively young people who belong to the age group 25-34 may have changed in language behaviour to increase the feeling of identification with the larger society. Older age groups may not have this aptitude and may have been too old to change their behaviour.

In the case of the Japanese, the pattern of language spoken at home is different. As age increases, the proportion who can speak their ethnic language at home increases systematically. However, the percentages are not significantly different between the two young age groups. Of the people who are 65 and older, more than 77 percent speak Japanese at home. Most of the Japanese belonging to the 0-4 and 25-34 age groups are Canadians by birth; it is natural for them to speak the local language even though their parents or grandparents, who may have been first generation immigrants to Canada, prefer to speak Japanese at home.

The comparison of Chinese and Japanese patterns of language spoken at home by age is indicative of a degree of acculturation. The much lower percentages of ethnic language maintenance among Japanese in the younger age groups implies the importance of place of birth variable. Seventy-five percent of the Japanese in Canada are native born and have generally experienced a greater degree of contact with the English or French majority languages than those born outside Canada, and they have a greater tendency to speak these languages in the home.

The language categories considered for East Indians are "East Indian" and "other." These two categories fail to indicate the true language spoken at home. In India, where most of these immigrants come from, there is no universal language spoken at home. There are nearly twenty official languages besides dialects in the Indian subcontinent. Hence, unless one knows what languages are included in the first category of Table 2.12, it is difficult to make any inferences regarding the language spoken at home. It is possible that the "other" language category might have included other East Indian languages, and hence it constitutes larger percentages.

2.4 CONCLUSIONS

The historical review of Asian ethnic groups in Canada demonstrates that their historical experience in this country has been a difficult one, especially before the World War II period. Each ethnic group has experienced inequality of treatment in many areas such as employment, public accommodation, and services. The pre-World War II Canadian immigration policies were based on race, region, and cultural background instead of the potential economic contribution of the immigrants to Canadian society. In many respects, Asian labourers were exploited and misused by Canadian contractors. Though the Canadian government is now making an effort to check for inequality of treatment of minorities in Canada by establishing the Human Rights Commission, a climate of racism seems to be still prevalent as a significant number of cases of prejudice and discrimination have been reported to the commission (Bowerman, 1980). The recent immigration policies have been intended to be fair and objective, yet some discretionary powers in the hands of immigration officers may be exercised against potential non-white immigrants. In sum, Asians in Canada do not enjoy the powers and privileges of complete citizenship in every aspect of Canadian life, particularly in the economic and political spheres.

Regarding data on background characteristics of Asian ethnic groups, differences are observed. These differences seem to be correlated with their duration of stay in Canada and the influence of historical factors. Historically, the Japanese and the Chinese entered different occupations in Canada (the majority of Chinese concentrated in service categories, Japanese in managerial and teaching categories), in part because of the different opportunities available to the two groups. This is also supported by Li (1979) who found that the heavy concentration of the Chinese in service industries such as laundrymen and restaurant workers, for example, was largely a result of restricted opportunities in the non-ethnic sector. These unequal opportunity structures to which these groups were subjected resulted in differences in socio-economic achievements (Li, 1980). The recency of East Indian immigration seems to be associated with their higher educational qualifications and greater concentration in science and medicine and also a more equalitarian distribution of wealth. To the income disparity between the Chinese and the Japanese, variations in educational attainment and in job characteristics seem to be contributing, besides historical factors. As far as acculturation is concerned, the duration of stay in Canada seems to be an important factor. If the language spoken at home is any indication of assimilation, the Japanese immigrants are better adapted than the other two groups. This may be because a substantial number of the Chinese and East Indian immigrants are recent arrivals. This is also reflected by their young age structure and concentration in urban areas.

To re-capitulate what we have said so far in view of the objective of the study: The major Asian ethnic groups have had different historical experiences in Canada and display different characteristics along the dimensions of education, occupation, and acculturation. The historical factors, which are associated with a discriminatory immigration system, seems to have played an important role in the present demographic structures of the Asian ethnic groups. For example, the small volume of Japanese immigration to Canada in the post-war period (only 25 percent of the Japanese are foreign born) greatly altered the demographic and social characteristics of the Japanese community (Ujimoto, 1976). In the case of the United States, Rindfuss and Sweet (1977) have shown that fluctuations in black-white fertility since 1920 were produced by the historical factors. Rindfuss (1980) also emphasizes that one has to take into account the socio-economic and historical factors and also other variables that have produced differential fertility among these groups. If this is the case, the history of Asian ethnic groups and the presentation of their socio-economic disparities should help us to understand the fertility patterns of these groups in Canada.

3
Asian Ethnic
Fertility Differentials

As we have indicated in the introductory chapter, the main thrust of the thesis is to first document the fertility differentials of Asian ethnic groups and then investigate possible sources of variation. In addition, the minority group status perspective will be used to attempt to explain family size differences. The purpose of this chapter is to document the fertility patterns and family sizes of Asian ethnic groups using 1971 census unpublished data and to look at how ethnic background affects fertility behaviour. Differences in fertility are often conditioned by variations in the proportion of people marrying, their age at marriage, and the duration of marriage. In societies where fertility is mainly within marriage, it is possible to divide the overall fertility into two components: marital fertility and nuptiality (Coale, 1969). In the case of Asian ethnic groups in Canada, it can be said that marriage signals the initiation of childbearing. Hence, fertility analysis in this chapter will take into account age at marriage, marriage duration, and marital fertility.

The average family sizes in 1971 of Asian ethnic groups by age and age at marriage are shown in Tables 3.1 and 3.2, respectively. The average number of children born to all Asians is 2.29. The comparison of this figure by ethnic background indicates that the Chinese maintain the largest family size, the East Indians the smallest family size, and the Japanese intermediate family size. When we control for age, the pattern does not remain the same at every age group. The Chinese have the highest fertility, the Japanese have the lowest fertility, and the East Indians are between the two. However, when the age at marriage is controlled, the situation seems similar to the one observed when there was no control for age. Among those married at a younger age, the Japanese have the highest average number of children. For those who were married in the age group of 20-24 or older, we again have

TABLE 3.1
Average Number of Children for Asian Women by Present Age
of Women for the Four Asian Ethnic Groups, Canada, 1971

Age Group	Chinese	Japanese	East Indians	Other Asian	Total
15-19	0.60	0.28	0.46	0.36	0.46
20-24	0.95	0.60	0.72	0.81	0.81
25-29	1.48	1.02	1.23	1.34	1.31
30-34	2.43	1.79	1.89	2.06	2.14
35-39	3.16	2.34	2.61	2.64	2.81
40-44	3.52	2.47	3.11	2.90	3.08
45-49	3.31	2.61	3.39	3.12	3.09
Total	2.55	2.36	1.85	2.23	2.29

Source: Unpublished 1971 census data of Canada.

TABLE 3.2
Average Number of Children for Asian Women by Age at
Marriage of Women for the Four Asian Ethnic Groups,
Canada, 1971

Age Group	Chinese	Japanese	East Indians	Other Asians	Total
15-19	3.16	3.70	2.66	2.94	3.04
20-24	2.49	2.47	1.78	2.22	2.27
25-29	2.01	1.99	1.39	1.84	1.82
30+	1.59	1.40	1.09	1.39	1.39
Total	2.55	2.36	1.85	2.23	2.29

Source: Unpublished 1971 census data of Canada.

the pattern of Chinese, Japanese, and East Indians in decreasing order of fertility.

Table 3.3 presents the average family sizes for the four categories when both age and age at marriage are controlled. The conclusions we can draw from this table are important and interesting. Once age at marriage is controlled, the patterns of fertility by age for the three ethnic categories are not the same as in Table 3.1. Generally speaking, for all ages at marriage, the Japanese are the ones showing the lowest family sizes. The comparison between the Chinese and the East Indian fertility patterns by age for the age at marriage group of 15-19 years is different from other older ages at marriage. For the group with 15-19 years as age of marriage, family sizes tend to be higher for the Chinese in the younger age groups, but the reverse is the case for older age groups. For older ages at marriage, the Chinese maintain consistently higher fertility than the East Indians. Another general observation is that as age at marriage increases the fertility decreases for all the groups regardless of the present age of the women. Thus, with a few exceptions the pattern is of increasing fertility from Japanese, to East Indians, to Chinese.

3.1 PARITY SPECIFIC FERTILITY ANALYSIS

The fertility process is characterized by two parameters, namely the quantum and the tempo. The quantum refers to the number of births occurring to the cohort, and the tempo refers to the timing of births within the reproductive cycle. In this section we will confine ourselves mainly to the study of the regulation of the quantum of fertility of Asian ethnic groups. This will help us to understand the changes in reproductive behaviour of these ethnic groups.

The traditional fertility measures used in the demographic analysis are crude birth rate, total fertility rate, gross reproduction rate, net reproduction rate, and an intrinsic rate of natural increase with regard to completed fertility. These measures make no reference either to the order of birth or to the parity of women. The fertility process is susceptible to the distributional distortion of births, so any conclusions based on these measures can be misleading (Wunsch and Termote, 1978). Unless the fertility measures are computed based on order of birth and parity of women, it is difficult to make any observations regarding the variation of fecundity and fertility of women.

As Ryder (1982) indicates, the main idea of regulation of the quantum of fertility is to examine the termination of childbearing at a particular parity, that is to consider the difference between fertility at one parity and fertility at the next conditional on the attained parity. The study of quantum regulation thus concentrates on parity-dependent

TABLE 3.3
Average Number of Children Born for Asian Women by Age at
First Marriage, Present Age, Canada, 1971

Age at First Marriage and Present Age		Chinese	Japanese	East Indians	Other Asians	Total Asians
15-19						
	15-19	0.60	0.28	0.46	0.36	0.46
	20-24	1.56	1.57	1.13	1.28	1.34
	25-29	2.57	2.31	2.24	2.45	2.41
	30-34	3.39	2.73	2.94	2.93	3.14
	35-39	3.63	3.13	3.77	3.38	3.61
	40-44	4.22	3.16	3.91	4.11	4.08
	45-49	4.31	3.23	4.41	4.15	4.19
20-24						
	15-19	-	-	-	-	-
	20-24	0.60	0.40	0.50	0.51	0.53
	25-29	1.55	1.17	1.35	1.35	1.40
	30-34	2.75	2.20	2.35	2.36	2.52
	35-39	3.42	2.62	2.80	2.88	3.05
	40-44	3.67	2.78	3.34	3.20	3.28
	45-49	3.47	2.88	3.62	3.33	3.28
25-29						
	15-19	-	-	-	-	-
	20-24	-	-	-	-	-
	25-29	0.56	0.36	0.49	0.52	0.50
	30-34	1.67	1.28	1.39	1.40	1.50
	35-39	2.76	2.26	2.35	2.41	2.50
	40-44	2.89	2.53	2.80	2.37	2.66
	45-49	2.74	2.55	2.61	2.74	2.67
30+						
	15-19	-	-	-	-	-
	20-24	-	-	-	-	-
	25-29	-	-	-	-	-
	30-34	0.85	0.79	0.50	0.61	0.64
	35-39	1.36	1.11	1.14	1.28	1.23
	40-44	2.00	1.58	1.48	1.32	1.63
	45-49	1.65	1.70	2.03	1.78	1.74
Total		2.55	2.36	1.85	2.23	2.29

Source: Unpublished 1971 census data of Canada.

reproduction behaviour. Quantum regulation has a proportional effect on all fertility beyond the parity in question but no effect on fertility prior to that parity. It also requires consideration of reproductive behaviour parity by parity rather than a fertility measure that has no reference to birth order (Ryder, 1982).

Parity Progression Ratios

The term parity refers to the number of live births a woman has. A woman with zero parity has had no live births, and a first parity woman has had one live birth. The computation of parity progression ratios requires the distribution of mothers by birth order. The procedure adopted here is the one used by Pressat (1972). Let X_1 be the number of women with at least one live-born child and X_2 be the number of women with at least two live-born children, then the ratio X_2/X_1 gives the proportion of women who have had at least two children among women who have had at least one child. This ratio is denoted by a_1. Similar ratios at different birth orders are also calculated.

Another method of calculating the parity progression ratios involves using the specific birth cohorts by marriage cohorts. This approach has an advantage over the other which has no reference to either age or marriage cohorts, since it distinguishes the variations in the "marriage-mix," i.e., the variations from cohort to cohort in the relative proportions of females marrying at specified ages (Wunsch and Termote, 1978). Moreover this type of study is useful in identifying distributional distortions of births due to the cohort tempo of births, that is the timing of births which differs from one birth cohort to another. Whelpton (1946) demonstrated this point while he was computing birth order specific fertility measures for white American female cohorts. He was of the opinion that the age-parity specific birth rates are better measures of fertility simply because the computed birth performance prior to a given age of women in a hypothetical cohort will differ in most cases from the actual birth performances prior to the same age of the women in the actual population. Both the cohorts, the hypothetical and the actual, will yield same values for fertility measures if there was no change in the timing of the births among the two cohorts. This is important because fertility at a given age is affected by fertility at younger ages. For example, if higher order births are being observed, it is quite likely that the women in question started their reproduction at early ages. The age-parity specific birth rates for a given year give proper weight to the fertility in prior years of each age cohort in the actual population, and hence they measure more accurately than age specific rates (Whelpton, 1946).

The parity progression ratios by age groups are presented in Table 3.4. This table shows that, within each of the age

TABLE 3.4
Parity Progression Ratios for Different
Age Groups by Ethnicity

Ethnicity by Age Group		a_0	a_1	a_2	a_3	a_4	a_5
Chinese	15-19	0.516	0.188	0.333	0	0	0
Japanese	15-19	0.200	0	0	0	0	0
East Indians	15-19	0.400	0.188	0	0	0	0
Other Asians	15-19	0.313	0.200	0	0	0	0
Chinese	20-24	0.590	0.467	0.270	0.129	0.500	0.500
Japanese	20-24	0.471	0.250	0.300	0	0	0
East Indians	20-24	0.524	0.305	0.186	0.076	1	0
Other Asians	20-24	0.523	0.375	0.235	0.333	0.25	0
Chinese	25-29	0.721	0.629	0.451	0.319	0.283	0.462
Japanese	25-29	0.615	0.489	0.277	0.222	0.500	0.500
East Indians	25-29	0.705	0.513	0.321	0.315	0.179	0
Other Asians	25-29	0.713	0.551	0.323	0.328	0.435	0.100
Chinese	30-34	0.889	0.845	0.613	0.452	0.361	0.387
Japanese	30-34	0.832	0.687	0.426	0.328	0.263	0.200
East Indians	30-34	1.821	0.712	0.496	0.404	0.410	0.344
Other Asians	30-34	0.849	0.779	0.550	0.342	0.372	0.316
Chinese	35-39	0.946	0.912	0.750	0.595	0.483	0.468
Japanese	35-39	0.901	0.834	0.597	0.350	0.395	0.176
East Indians	35-39	0.863	0.862	0.684	0.527	0.406	0.488
Other Asians	35-39	0.909	0.871	0.625	0.524	0.420	0.432
Chinese	40-44	0.941	0.916	0.830	0.679	0.581	0.496
Japanese	40-44	0.848	0.857	0.656	0.524	0.406	0.385
East Indians	40-44	0.911	0.881	0.743	0.630	0.613	0.531
Other Asians	40-44	0.894	0.886	0.668	0.608	0.461	0.543
Chinese	45-49	0.908	0.895	0.789	0.670	0.621	0.517
Japanese	45-49	0.876	0.858	0.656	0.524	0.426	0.478
East Indians	45-49	0.906	0.883	0.794	0.611	0.727	0.625
Other Asians	45-49	0.907	0.888	0.672	0.610	0.587	0.682

Source: Computed from unpublished 1971 census data of Canada.

groups, the Chinese maintain the highest parity progression ratios when compared to the other groups, and this is more or less true for all the age groups and across all birth orders. The East Indians come next, and the Japanese occupy the lowest rank in their progression to higher parities. The analysis of parity progression ratios contradicts an earlier observation made based on Table 3.2 that the Japanese women maintain intermediate fertility compared to the Chinese and the East Indians. The parity progression ratios indicate that the East Indians are intermediate in their fertility behaviour and that the Japanese are maintaining smaller family sizes compared to the other two categories of ethnicity. This inference is in agreement with Table 3.3 in which we studied family sizes by controlling for both age and age at marriage.

As indicated earlier, these parity progression ratios are also calculated by marriage cohorts and are presented in Table 3.5. The Chinese still maintain the pattern observed

TABLE 3.5
Parity Progression Ratios for Different Marriage
Cohorts by Ethnicity

Ethnicity	Age Group	a_0	a_1	a_2	a_3	a_4	a_5
Chinese	15-19	0.946	0.858	0.738	0.627	0.548	0.554
Japanese	15-19	0.954	0.876	0.828	0.681	0.663	0.607
East Indians	15-19	0.866	0.816	0.650	0.613	0.541	0.557
Other Asians	15-19	0.897	0.829	0.672	0.619	0.569	0.646
Chinese	20-24	0.849	0.811	0.663	0.564	0.500	0.516
Japanese	20-24	0.849	0.799	0.650	0.559	0.510	0.519
East Indians	20-24	0.769	0.650	0.534	0.463	0.493	0.521
Other Asians	20-24	0.808	0.782	0.587	0.522	0.500	0.549
Chinese	25-29	0.801	0.850	0.559	0.471	0.451	0.420
Japanese	25-29	0.774	0.782	0.579	0.442	0.382	0.379
East Indians	25-29	0.698	0.566	0.431	0.384	0.395	0.471
Other Asians	25-29	0.769	0.704	0.521	0.480	0.431	0.484
Chinese	30+	0.702	0.621	0.539	0.520	0.487	0.421
Japanese	30+	0.705	0.589	0.487	0.324	0.250	0.667
East Indians	30+	0.575	0.471	0.462	0.433	0.538	0.571
Other Asians	30+	0.639	0.641	0.462	0.326	0.571	0.750

Source: Computed from unpublished 1971 data of Canada on birth order.

earlier of having the highest fertility, but, for the other two groups, the pattern of ratios does not remain the same as those shown in Table 3.4. We now see the Japanese as having the intermediate while the East Indians are the lowest. In summary, it can be said that when age is controlled the East Indians tend to maintain higher levels of fertility than the Japanese, which is in accordance with the earlier inference, but when age at marriage is controlled the situation reverses. The reasons for these contradictions will be discussed in the following paragraphs.

The fertility analysis presented so far for the Asian ethnic groups clearly shows that when age patterns of fertility are studied, the East Indians show consistently higher family sizes than the Japanese, but when duration of marriage is considered instead of age, the situation reverses. Even when age at marriage is controlled to examine family sizes by age groups, it is difficult to arrive at any definitive conclusions. In the absence of any control for socio-economic characteristics, the possible explanation lies in the nature of the age structure. It is possible to see from Table 2.4, showing ethnic groups by age, that East Indians form the younger age distribution followed by the Chinese and then the Japanese. This can be highlighted by the following summary figures on the age structure computed from unpublished data:

Age	Chinese	Japanese	East Indian	Other Asian
Below 35	39%	28%	65%	41%
Above 35	61%	72%	35%	59%

It is possible to argue from the above percentages that the East Indians, because of their young age structure, might not have completed their intended family sizes, and hence the comparison of the three groups makes sense only among those who have completed their reproductive period, i.e., controlling for age.

It also does not seem to be appropriate to compare the family sizes of the Asian ethnic origin groups by age at marriage groups. It is quite likely that the East Indians have a shorter duration of marriage compared to either the Japanese or the Chinese considering the period from age at marriage to the census date. In other words, this is a truncation bias. This is even more serious than the comparison of fertility based on age groups. Table 3.3 does take into account age and age at marriage simultaneously, but the family size differences that are observed between groups by age may be temporary, especially among the younger women, as they might not have completed their family sizes. Thus a useful comparison is possible only for the women who have completed their reproductive period by birth order. In the following section, we will consider women who are in the age group 45-49 and try to distribute these women by birth order using the life table approach.

Life Table Approach

While it is analogous to a life table in the study of the mortality process, the preparation of a reproduction table in fertility is not a popular procedure because age specific birth rates cannot be used in the preparation of an attrition table. Death, being an irreversible event, can be studied fairly easily by life table. However, fecundity and fertility of women vary widely, as some people cannot have a child, many have two or three, and a very few have twenty or more (Whelpton, 1946). If one wants to calculate a reproduction table, the relationship between parity of women and birth order of children needs to be considered. Zero parity women can have only first births, second births can occur only to first parity women, and so on. In general terms only the women of 'n' parity can be exposed to the risk of bearing a child of n + 1 order (Whelpton, 1946).

Like Pressat (1972) we will use the parity progression ratios already calculated in Tables 3.4 and 3.5 in order to compute the manner in which different family sizes are distributed for a radix of 1000 women.

Let us consider the parity progression ratios of the Chinese women who have completed their fertility from Table 3.4.

The figure for Chinese women $a_0 = 0.908$ indicates that of 1000 women, 908 have had at least one child and the remaining 92 have had no children. Similarly, $a_1 = 0.895$ indicates that among the 908 women who have had at least one child, 812.7 (908 x 0.895 = 812.7) have had at least two children, while the remaining 95.3 women had exactly one child. Further, $a_2 = 0.789$ indicates that among the 812.7 women who have had at least two children (812.7 x 0.789 = 641.2), 641.2 have had at least three children and the remaining 171.5 have had exactly two children, and so on.

This calculation can be carried out in a systematic fashion as below.

Among 1000 Chinese women who are in the age group 45-49:

1000	100.0 had at least 0 children
1000x0.908	908.0 had at least 1 child
1000x0.908x0.895	812.7 had at least 2 children
1000x0.908x0.895x0.789	641.2 had at least 3 children
1000x0.908x0.895x0.789x0.670	429.6 had at least 4 children
1000x0.908x0.895x0.789x0.670x0.621	266.8 had at least 5 children
1000x0.908x0.895x0.789x0.670x0.621x0.517	137.9 had at least 6 children

By successive subtractions among the same 1000 women it also follows:

1000.0 - 908.0 = 92.0 had zero children

908.0 - 812.7 = 95.3 had one child

812.7 - 641.2 = 171.5 had two children

641.2 - 429.6 = 211.6 had three children

429.6 - 266.8 = 162.8 had four children

266.8 - 137.9 = 128.9 had five children

137.9 had six or more children

Thus the 1,000 women can be distributed by number of children. We admit that this distribution, which is based on a life table approach, is a roundabout procedure, however, its convenience is that we have here a radix of 1,000 which makes comparison easier. The distribution for the four categories of the Asian women who have completed their fertility is as follows:

	Number of Children						
Ethnicity	0	1	2	3	4	5	6+
Chinese	92	95	172	212	163	129	138
Japanese	124	124	259	235	148	58	53
East Indians	94	106	165	247	106	106	176
Other Asians	93	102	264	211	136	62	132

By comparing the four ethnic categories we can say that more than 12 percent of the Japanese ever-married women are childless; in the other categories, only about 9 percent are childless. This might be one of the contributing factors to the low fertility of Japanese women. Another observation we can make is that the modal value for the Japanese women is two children, whereas for the Chinese and the East Indians the corresponding value is three children. We can also see that only 5 percent of the Japanese women have six or more children, compared to nearly 14 and 18 percent of the Chinese and East Indian women, respectively. We may summarize that the lower fertility of Japanese older women could be due to a higher proportion of childlessness and a lower proportional representation of women in higher parities among other (unknown) factors.

Following the above procedure and using the parity progression ratios shown in Table 3.5, Table 3.6 was computed.

TABLE 3.6
Distribution of 1000 Women by Number of Children Born by
Marriage Cohorts Based on Parity Progression Ratios

Ethnicity	Age at Marriage	Number of Children						
		0	1	2	3	4	5	6+
Chinese	15-19	54	134	213	223	170	92	114
Japanese	15-19	46	118	144	221	159	123	190
East Indians	15-19	134	159	240	181	131	69	86
Other Asians	15-19	103	153	244	190	133	62	114
Chinese	20-24	151	161	232	199	129	62	66
Japanese	20-24	151	171	237	195	121	61	65
East Indians	20-24	231	269	233	143	63	29	32
Other Asians	20-24	192	176	261	177	97	44	53
Chinese	25-29	199	200	265	178	87	41	30
Japanese	25-29	226	169	255	196	96	37	22
East Indians	25-29	302	303	225	105	40	14	12
Other Asians	25-29	231	228	259	147	77	30	28
Chinese	30+	298	266	201	113	63	34	25
Japanese	30+	295	290	213	137	49	6	11
East Indians	30+	425	304	146	71	25	13	17
Other Asians	30+	361	229	220	128	27	9	26

Source: Computed from Table 3.5.

This table presents the distribution of 1,000 women by number of children controlling for marriage cohorts. This gives a completely different picture of the situation. Among all the marriage cohorts, the East Indian women appear in higher proportion than the Chinese and the Japanese among the childless couples. However, the proportion of childless couples increases as age at marriage increases. The modal values for the 15-19 years of age at marriage cohorts are three children for the Chinese and the Japanese but two children for the East Indian women. Then, for the age at marriage cohorts 20-24 years and 25-29 years, the modal values are two children for the Chinese and Japanese, but one child for the East Indians. Thus, a higher proportion of couples are having higher order births among the Chinese and the Japanese compared to the East Indians, except for the last age at marriage group, where the East Indians maintain a higher proportion of couples at higher birth orders.

The fertility analysis presented so far for the Asian ethnic groups clearly shows that both age and age at marriage are important sources of fertility variation. Though age may be a variable for the specification of a pattern of fertility, it is still inadequate because the age at which women begin childbearing can vary. Page (1977) argues that physiological factors are not only related to age but to marriage duration as well. Fecundity may vary with marriage duration, irrespective of age. Furthermore, under conditions of changing fertility the various marriage and birth cohorts may react differently. Page (1977) also explains how differentials in fertility behaviour by age at marriage may affect both age as well as marriage duration. For example, if those who marry younger have higher fertility, then the younger women in every marriage duration group will show higher fertility rates, relative to the older women in their duration group, than is accounted for simply by their age. Similarly, in a given age, the women who have been married longest are those who married youngest; hence, they will show higher fertility rates relative to those who married more recently than is accounted for simply by their marriage duration. This is why we will study the relative contribution of age and marriage duration in the differential fertility of Asian ethnic groups in the following section.

3.2 FERTILITY DECOMPOSITION BY BOTH AGE AND MARRIAGE DURATION

Identification of patterns in mortality, nuptiality, and fertility by Coale and his associates have been very important and useful for development in recent demographic research (Coale and Demeny, 1966; Coale, 1971; Coale and Trussel, 1974). These models, which were purely based on age, especially in fertility, were criticized by some researchers (e.g., Page, 1977). A more fruitful model was developed by Page (1977), which takes into account both age and marital duration. Her reason for developing such a model was that

> Age cannot bear the same relation to fertility experience in all populations, because the age at which women begin childbearing can vary widely. For populations in which childbearing occurs predominantly within marriage, duration of marriage is a more direct specification than age for detecting patterns of control. (Page, 1977: 86-87)

She is also aware of the fact that duration alone is not sufficient as age also controls childbearing, so the model she has proposed is based on both age and marriage duration. Moreover she has successfully demonstrated that her model not only fits the data better than the one based solely on age, but also penetrates deeper into the structures underlying fertility schedules and, as a result, is more revealing.

An attempt has been made to use the model specified by Page (1977) in order to decompose the fertility of Asian women into age and marital duration and to observe any underlying patterns that may prevail. The model is briefly described and its parameters are discussed. Let us start with the equation of the model that is

$$m(a,d,t) = L(t) \cdot V(a,t) \cdot U(d,t)$$

Where $m(a,d,t)$ is the marital fertility rate for women at age a, marriage duration d, and time t
$L(t)$ is the general level of marital fertility at time t, averaged over all ages and marriage durations
$V(a,t)$ is a factor characteristic of age a at time t
$U(d,t)$ is a factor characteristic of duration d at time t.

The vector $V(a,t)$ represents an age pattern shared by all marriage cohorts at time t, and the vector $U(d,t)$ is a duration pattern shared by all age groups. Note that the model is multiplicative in nature meaning that

> the extreme situation would arise if fertility varied exponentially with age at marriage..., all the age at marriage effect would automatically be included in both the $V(a,t)$ and the $U(d,t)$ estimates and there would be no distinctive pattern of residuals left to indicate its existence. If an age at marriage effect exists but is not completely exponential then any exponential element will be included in the $V(a,t)$ and $U(d,t)$ estimates, but the remainder will appear as a concentration of residuals in certain age and marriage duration combinations. (Page, 1977:90)

The method of estimation adopted here for the model's parameters is slightly different from the one used by Page (1977) due to different circumstances. The data must be presented in a two-way table for an estimate of overall average value $L(t)$ and row and column affects $V(a,t)$ and $U(d,t)$ to be made. Page's two-way table contained extreme values in the tails of the distribution, and, hence, instead of calculating a mean of all observations in a row, she used a procedure referred to as "trimmed mean polish" to calculate a mean that is unaffected by extreme values (Page, 1977). In our case, the values are approximately uniformly distributed, and due to fewer observations, the mean of all the observations is calculated in both rows and columns.

Since the model is multiplicative, for the sake of convenience, logarithmic transformations were made of the observed ratio, and a mean was calculated for each row and is seen as a typical value for that row. For each row, residuals from their typical values are calculated. A typical value for the whole table is also calculated as the mean of the row typical values, and what is left when this general typical value is subtracted from the row typicals are the row effects. The row effects, converted back from logarithms, are the duration effects or the duration vector $U(d,t)$. Similarly, to calculate the age vector $V(a,t)$, the mean of the residuals within each column is extracted as the column effect. By converting these column effects back from logarithms, we would get the age effects. The procedure is repeated for all the ethnic groups of Asian origin. The actual calculations are presented in Tables 3.7 to 3.10.

The Age Patterns and Age Effects

In situations of natural fertility, that is, in situations where there is no deliberate birth control, age patterns of fertility should be essentially similar because of physiological reasons. Henry (1961) in fact found such regularity in populations where there is no voluntary control of births. Coale and Trussel (1974) developed model fertility schedules in which they showed that marital fertility either follows natural fertility, if no deliberate birth control is practiced, or departs from natural fertility in a way that increases with age according to a typical pattern.

In Figure 3.1 we can see the underlying age patterns of fertility of Asian ethnic groups. It is interesting to see that these vectors are all of a single basic shape although they differ slightly in their steepness. As far as the age effect is concerned, it appears that, among all Asian origin groups, couples become voluntarily less fertile as age increases. The marital fertility diminishes constantly with age for all groups except for the Chinese. In the Chinese case, there is a tendency toward a small, almost negligible, increase at the end of the reproductive period.

The comparison of age effects between the Japanese and the East Indians is interesting. At younger ages, the age effects are more prominent for the East Indians but, at older ages, for the Japanese. We hypothesize that the young age structure of the East Indians should account for at least part of the age effect differences between the Japanese and the East Indians. It is possible to find more older Japanese women with longer duration of stay in Canada with completed family sizes than their East Indian counterparts. The historical review of these groups presented in an earlier chapter indicates that there have been very few Japanese immigrants to Canada in recent years. As far as the steepness of the age effects vector is concerned, it decreases for all the ethnic groups up to the age group 35-39 and tends to stabilize thereafter. In conclusion, we may say that age differentiates fertility behaviour among the Asian ethnic groups and its effect decreases as age increases.

TABLE 3.7
Logarithms of Age Specific Marital Fertility Rates by Age and Marriage Duration (per 1,000) of Chinese Women

Marriage Duration	Age						Row Means	Row Effects	Antilog of Row Effects U(d)
	20-24	25-29	30-34	35-39	40-44	45-49			
0- 4	3.19394	3.40194	3.52288	3.55091	3.60907	3.60791	3.48111	-0.17565	0.66734
5- 9	2.82552	3.19126	3.43783	3.52677	3.55032	3.53387	3.34426	-0.03880	0.91453
10-14	-	2.74673	3.22186	3.44125	3.46107	3.43366	3.26091	0.04455	1.10803
15+	-	-	2.88081	3.13225	3.31315	3.21601	3.13556	0.16991	1.47880

Marriage Duration	Age					
	20-24	25-29	30-34	35-39	40-44	45-49
0- 4	0.28717	0.07917	-0.04177	-0.06980	-0.12796	-0.12680
5- 9	0.51874	0.153	-0.09357	-0.18251	-0.20606	-0.18961
10-14	-	0.51418	0.03905	-0.18034	-0.20016	-0.17275
15+	-	-	0.25475	0.00331	-0.17759	-0.08045
Column Effects	0.40295	0.24878	0.03961	-0.10734	-0.17795	-0.14240
Antilog of Column Effects V(t)	2.52901	1.77329	1.09549	0.78102	0.66382	0.72042

Source: Computed from unpublished 1971 census data of Canada on fertility rates.

TABLE 3.8

Logarithms of Age Specific Marital Fertility Rates by Age and Marriage Duration (per 1,000) of Japanese Women

Marriage Duration	Age						Row Means	Row Effects	Antilog of Row Effects U(t)
	20-24	25-29	30-34	35-39	40-44	45-49			
0- 4	3.20412	3.39334	3.40458	3.50515	3.50515	3.49291	3.41754	-0.19627	0.63640
5- 9	2.60831	3.06458	3.33943	3.41795	3.43531	3.44425	3.21831	0.00296	1.00684
10-14	-	2.54881	3.11856	3.34803	3.39237	3.39794	3.16114	0.06013	1.14850
15+	-	-	2.87506	3.04015	3.19782	3.23938	3.08810	0.13318	1.35888

Marriage Duration	Age					
	20-24	25-29	30-34	35-39	40-44	45-49
0- 4	0.21342	0.0242	0.01296	-0.08761	-0.08761	-0.07537
5- 9	0.61	0.15373	-0.12112	-0.19964	-0.217	-0.22594
10-14	-	0.61233	0.04258	-0.18689	-0.23123	-0.23680
15+	-	-	0.21304	-0.04795	-0.10972	-0.15127
Column Effects	0.41171	0.26342	0.03687	-0.10655	-0.16139	-0.17235
Antilog of Column Effects V(t)	2.58054	1.83409	1.08860	0.78244	0.68962	0.67243

Source: Computed from unpublished 1971 census data of Canada on fertility rates.

TABLE 3.9
Logarithms of Age Specific Marital Fertility Rates by Age and Marriage Duration (per 1,000) of East Indian Women

Marriage Duration	Age						Row Means	Row Effects	Antilog of Row Effects U(t)
	20-24	25-29	30-34	35-39	40-44	45-49			
0- 4	3.04922	3.35289	3.45962	3.56340	3.58723	3.59770	3.43501	-0.19035	0.64513
5- 9	2.69436	3.13004	3.36709	3.44321	3.51087	3.55396	3.28326	-0.0386	0.91496
10-14	-	2.70240	3.13973	3.37323	3.44369	3.44494	3.22080	0.02306	1.05453
15+	-	-	2.69417	3.06611	3.14613	3.25182	3.03956	0.2051	1.60361

Marriage Duration	Age					
	20-24	25-29	30-34	35-39	40-44	45-49
0- 4	0.38579	0.08212	-0.02461	-0.12839	-0.15222	-0.16269
5- 9	0.5889	0.15322	-0.08383	-0.15995	-0.22761	-0.2707
10-14	-	0.5184	0.08107	-0.15243	-0.22289	-0.22415
15+	-	-	0.34539	-0.02655	-0.10657	-0.21226
Column Effects	0.48735	0.25125	0.07951	-0.11683	-0.17732	0.21745
Antilog of Column Effects V(t)	3.07149	1.78341	1.20091	0.76413	0.66478	0.60611

Source: Computed from unpublished 1971 census data of Canada on fertility rates.

TABLE 3.10

Logarithms of Age Specific Marital Fertility Rates by Age and Marriage Duration (per 1,000) of Other Asian Women

Marriage Duration	Age						Row Means	Row Effects	Antilog of Row Effects U(t)
	20-24	25-29	30-34	35-39	40-44	45-49			
0- 4	3.09949	3.38996	3.52170	3.50864	3.55931	3.56845	3.44126	-0.17954	0.66139
5- 9	2.66511	3.12770	3.69573	3.45564	3.49392	3.48903	3.32119	-0.05947	0.87203
10-14	-	2.72263	3.13594	3.37787	3.37107	3.42936	3.20737	0.05435	1.13331
15+	-	-	2.83863	3.09276	3.14780	3.22902	3.07705	0.18467	1.52992

Marriage Duration	Age					
	20-24	25-29	30-34	35-39	40-44	45-49
0- 4	0.34177	0.0513	-0.08044	-0.06738	-0.11805	-0.12719
5- 9	0.65608	0.19349	-0.37454	-0.13445	-0.17273	-0.16784
10-14	-	-.48474	0.07143	-0.1705	-0.1637	-0.22199
15+	-	-	0.23842	-0.01571	-0.07075	-0.15197
Column Effects	0.49893	0.24318	-0.03628	-0.09701	-0.13131	-0.16725
Antilog of Column Effects V(t)	3.15449	1.75057	0.91986	0.79982	0.73908	0.68038

Source: Computed from unpublished 1971 census data of Canada on fertility rates.

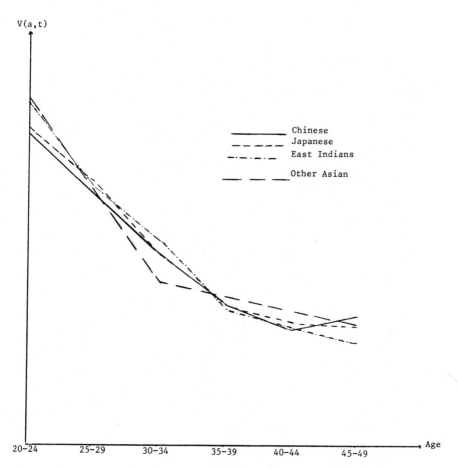

FIG 3.1: Distribution of Age Effects on Fertility of Asian Ethnic
Groups in Canada, 1971

Duration Patterns and Duration Effects

It can be said that fertility is related to both age and marital duration. In fact, marital duration can be more imporant than age in populations where contraceptives are widespread in explaining current fertility of couples, the reason being that most births occur at lower durations of marriage. Women aged 30, for example, will present eventual fertilities depending on their durations of marriage at that age (Wunsch and Termote, 1978).

In Figure 3.2, the duration effects of the four groups considered are shown. It is important to mention here that these effects are linear, and the three vectors show fairly straight lines except for the Japanese. The duration effect increases approximately at a constant rate, as the duration increases. The duration pattern of fertility differs from that of the age pattern discussed earlier. It would have been useful had there been an intuitively meaningful standard pattern external to our data to compare. It is also difficult to interpret the underlying patterns of our data. Page (1977) points out that, unlike age effects, the duration effects reveal no simple meaningful patterns in the cross-sectional form. However, it is very useful to consider marriage duration in the fertility analysis as Page has shown. Her model, including this feature, has reproduced the observed rates significantly better than the model based only on age. The conclusion we can draw from the duration effects in our case is that the cross-sectional duration effects do not seem to contribute to any irregularities in the fertility patterns.

In a sense, the above analysis, using a technique developed by Page for decomposing fertility schedules by both age and marriage duration, has involved a rather sophisticated procedure in order to obtain rather meager results. However, at least we are now confident that the basic demographic variables of age and duration of marriage are not confounding the fertility differences among the Asian ethnic groups. That is, these demographic variables operate basically in the same fashion in each of the groups.

3.3 FERTILITY BY PLACE OF BIRTH

In the post-war era, the foreign-born population of Canada has persistently experienced lower levels of reproduction in comparison to the native-born (Tracey, 1941; Charles, 1948; Krotki and Lapierre, 1968; Henripin, 1972; Balakrishnan et al., 1975; Balakrishnan et al., 1979; Collishaw, 1976; Kalbach and McVey, 1979; Richmond and Kalbach, 1980). Not only is this pattern well established nationally, but researchers on large metropolitan centres, such as Montreal and Toronto, have reasserted the persistence of lower foreign-born fertility (e.g., Balakrishnan et al., 1975; Balakrishnan et al., 1979; Richmond and Kalbach, 1980).

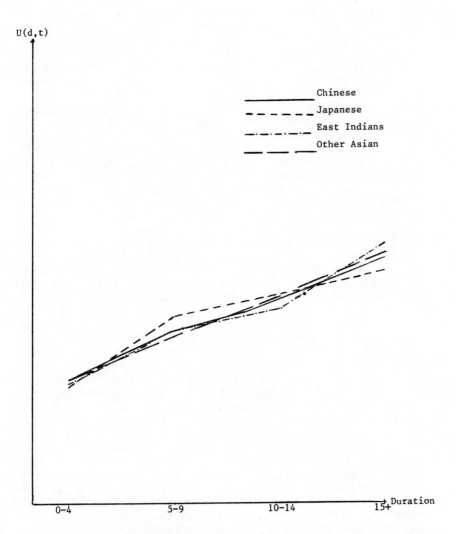

U(d,t)

Chinese
Japanese
East Indians
Other Asian

0-4   5-9   10-14   15+   Duration

FIG 3.2: Distribution of Duration Effects on Fertility of Asian Ethnic
Groups in Canada, 1971

Henripin (1972) used 1961 census data to explore the effect of endogamous marriage on childbearing among foreign- and native-born females. His conclusion was that regardless of whether the husband or the wife were of foreign status, the influence on childbearing is to reduce average family size below that of couples indigenous to this country:. . . the couples comprised of two native-born spouses stand out in marked contrast to the others by reason of their high fertility. (Henripin, 1972:150)

Balakrishnan and his associates (1979; 1975) in two separate studies, using the 1971 census and Toronto survey data, respectively, corroborate Henripin's earlier results. For the nation as a whole they asserted that: "Currently foreign-born women have much lower fertility than native-born women." (Balakrishnan et al. 1979:66) In Toronto, during the late 1960s, Balakrishnan et al. (1975), studied variations in the actual, expected, and desired family size among four nativity groups--Canadian born, Western European, Eastern European and residual category (other). Based on their results, they suggested that "...it would be advisable in future fertility research to give (nativity) greater consideration." (p. 34) Although the phenomenon in question has been observed on numerous occasions, no one has made an attempt to investigate fertility differentials among Asian ethnic groups by nativity. The essential problem under examination in this section is whether place of birth generates a difference in fertility behaviour.

Table 3.11 compares family sizes among four Asian ethnic groups by their place of birth. It is clear from the table that there are significant fertility differentials by place of birth for all groups listed in the table. The general conclusions drawn from the past research that foreign-born women maintain lower fertility than the native born does not always hold for Asian ethnic groups. What is more important to observe in regard to place of birth is in which country one was born. From Table 3.11, we can note that, in the case of the Chinese, those who were born in China had a higher fertility than the native born; but, in the case of those who were born in countries other than China, they have a lower fertility than the native -born. However, among the Japanese, native-born women have smaller families than those who are born in Asia and commonwealth countries (except the United Kingdom). Interestingly, the case of East Indians is peculiar in the sense that those East Indians who were born in China have a higher fertility rate than the rest, and those born in India and other south Asian countries seem to maintain their family sizes lower than the Canadian-born families.

Before we make any speculation about the contrasting results of ours with past research, it is important to provide an appropriate control for fertility such as age of the women and their age at marriage. In Tables 3.12 to 3.15 we can see the control of age and age at marriage to study the reproduction behaviour of four categories of Asian ethnic groups in Canada. When there was no control of age and age at

TABLE 3.11
Distribution of Average Number of Children Born to Ever Married
Women of Asian Ethnic Groups by Place of Birth, Canada, 1971

Birthplace	Ethnicity				
	Chinese	Japanese	East Indians	Other Asians	Total
Canada	2.35	2.34	2.32	2.35	2.35
United Kingdom	1.96	2.00	1.98	1.81	1.95
China	2.78	0.91	2.91	2.12	2.77
Other Asian Countries	1.99	2.44	1.80	2.30	2.04
Other Commonwealth Countries	1.77	3.58	2.02	1.88	1.86
Other Countries	2.15	2.07	1.61	1.93	1.91
Total Birthplace	2.55	2.36	1.85	2.23	2.29

Source: Unpublished 1971 census data of Canada.

Table 3.12
Average Number of Children Born for Chinese Women by Age at First
Marriage, Present Age and Birthplace, Canada, 1971

		Birthplace		
Age at First Marriage	Present Age	Canada	United Kingdom	China
15-19	15-19	0.39	--	0.68
	20-24	1.04	1.32	1.82
	25-29	2.17	--	2.71
	30-34	2.87	2.60	3.53
	35-39	3.59	4.60	3.62
	40-44	4.00	6.00	4.20
	45-49	4.64	--	4.18
20-24	15-19	--	--	--
	20-24	0.54	1.13	0.65
	25-29	1.50	1.73	1.70
	30-34	2.46	2.03	2.92
	35-39	2.87	3.33	3.58
	40-44	3.06	3.75	3.90
	45-49	3.21	6.00	3.64
25-29	15-19	--	--	--
	20-24	--	--	--
	25-29	0.42	0.42	0.62
	30-34	1.38	1.08	1.92
	35-39	2.34	2.30	2.98
	40-44	2.58	2.00	3.06
	45-49	2.71	--	2.88
30+	15-19	--	--	--
	20-24	--	--	--
	25-29	--	--	--
	30-34	0.15	--	1.07
	35-39	1.17	0.30	1.68
	40-44	2.18	0.80	2.08
	45-49	1.51	2.33	1.58

Source: Unpublished 1971 Census Data of Canada

Table 3.12
(continued)

| | Birthplace | | |
Other Asian Countries	Other Commonwealth Countries	Other Countries	Total
--	0.85	--	0.60
1.55	1.08	0.77	1.56
1.40	2.83	2.21	2.57
4.40	3.00	2.83	3.39
4.19	3.56	3.73	3.63
4.20	4.96	4.42	4.22
3.00	4.97	5.00	4.31
--	--	--	--
0.72	0.51	--	0.60
1.38	1.22	1.14	1.55
2.73	2.22	2.52	2.75
2.44	3.23	2.87	3.42
4.18	3.58	4.79	3.67
2.79	3.19	3.43	3.47
--	--	--	--
--	--	--	--
0.23	0.55	0.64	0.56
1.28	1.40	1.11	1.67
2.50	2.39	2.13	2.76
3.30	2.95	0.75	2.89
2.00	2.32	1.00	2.74
--	--	--	--
--	--	--	--
--	--	--	--
0.25	0.67	2.00	0.85
1.57	1.04	1.25	1.36
2.00	1.81	1.75	2.00
2.50	1.74	1.80	1.65

Table 3.13
Average Number of Children Born for Japanese Women by Age at First
Marriage, Present Age and Birthplace, Canada, 1971

Age at First Marriage	Present Age	Birthplace		
		Canada	United Kingdom	China
15-19	15-19	0.23	--	--
	20-24	1.57	--	--
	25-29	2.31	--	--
	30-34	2.79	--	--
	35-39	3.27	--	--
	40-44	3.41	--	--
	45-49	3.53	--	--
20-24	15-19	--	--	--
	20-24	0.39	--	--
	25-29	1.09	--	1.23
	30-34	2.28	--	1.00
	35-39	2.73	--	--
	40-44	3.00	2.40	--
	45-49	2.87	--	--
25-29	15-19	--	--	--
	20-24	--	--	--
	25-29	0.46	--	0.47
	30-34	1.31	--	1.00
	35-39	2.30	--	--
	40-44	2.61	--	--
	45-49	2.47	--	--
30+	15-19	--	--	--
	20-24	--	--	--
	25-29	--	--	--
	30-34	0.63	--	0.67
	35-39	1.25	--	--
	40-44	1.77	--	0.67
	45-49	1.87	--	--

Source: Unpublished 1971 Census Data of Canada

Table 3.13
(continued)

	Birthplace		
Other Asian Countries	Other Commonwealth Countries	Other Countries	Total
0.50	--	--	0.28
1.54	--	--	1.57
2.83	--	1.25	2.31
2.73	--	--	2.73
2.88	--	--	3.13
2.21	--	--	3.16
1.79	--	--	3.23
--	--	--	--
0.40	--	0.73	0.40
1.31	--	1.12	1.17
2.06	--	1.87	2.20
2.36	--	2.70	2.62
2.16	--	3.00	2.78
3.13	--	--	2.88
--	--	--	--
--	--	--	--
0.24	--	--	0.36
1.23	--	--	1.28
2.24	1.00	1.86	2.26
2.17	--	--	2.53
3.13	--	5.00	2.55
--	--	--	--
--	--	--	--
--	--	--	--
0.88	--	--	0.79
0.96	--	1.00	1.11
1.06	--	1.29	1.58
1.33	--	--	1.70

Table 3.14
Average Number of Children Born for East Indian Women by Age at First
Marriage, Present Age and Birthplace, Canada, 1971

Age at First Marriage	Present Age	Birthplace		
		Canada	United Kingdom	China
15-19	15-19	0.55	--	--
	20-24	0.85	2.00	--
	25-29	2.59	2.13	--
	30-34	3.20	2.71	6.00
	35-39	3.36	--	--
	40-44	4.43	--	7.00
	45-49	6.20	--	--
20-24	15-19	--	--	--
	20-24	0.47	0.50	--
	25-29	1.59	1.53	0.33
	30-34	2.41	2.67	2.14
	35-39	2.98	2.00	--
	40-44	3.22	1.00	--
	45-49	3.46	3.00	--
25-29	15-19	--	--	--
	20-24	--	--	--
	25-29	0.15	0.60	--
	30-34	1.46	1.67	--
	35-39	2.86	3.00	--
	40-44	2.64	--	--
	45-49	2.67	--	--
30+	15-19	--	--	--
	20-24	--	--	--
	25-29	--	--	--
	30-34	0.60	--	--
	35-39	1.86	2.20	--
	40-44	--	2.00	--
	45-49	0.78	--	--

Source: Unpublished 1971 Census Data of Canada

Table 3.14
(continued)

| | Birthplace | | |
Other Asian Countries	Other Commonwealth Countries	Other Countries	Total
0.51	0.32	--	0.46
1.10	1.25	1.20	1.13
2.20	2.29	2.22	2.24
2.92	3.01	2.41	2.94
3.76	4.32	3.00	3.77
3.84	3.81	3.16	3.91
4.28	3.25	7.80	4.41
--	--	--	--
0.52	0.44	0.33	0.50
1.34	1.39	1.25	1.35
2.31	2.64	2.13	2.35
2.78	3.41	1.98	2.80
3.30	4.03	3.56	3.34
3.44	5.09	3.00	3.62
--	--	--	--
--	--	--	--
0.51	0.35	0.63	0.49
1.37	1.67	1.03	1.39
2.34	2.50	1.61	2.35
2.77	3.33	2.50	2.80
2.55	3.00	2.00	2.61
--	--	--	--
--	--	--	--
--	--	--	--
0.49	0.61	0.62	0.50
1.16	0.43	0.86	1.14
1.41	1.97	0.70	1.48
1.50	6.10	--	2.03

Table 3.15
Average Number of Children Born for Other Asian Women by Age at First
Marriage, Present Age and Birthplace, Canada, 1971

Age at First Marriage	Present Age	Birthplace		
		Canada	United Kingdom	China
15-19	15-19	0.29	--	--
	20-24	1.25	1.40	--
	25-29	2.40	2.00	--
	30-34	2.83	2.00	--
	35-39	3.61	--	--
	40-44	3.74	--	--
	45-49	3.76	--	--
20-24	15-19	--	--	--
	20-24	0.33	--	--
	25-29	1.28	1.54	1.00
	30-34	2.57	2.43	2.43
	35-39	3.10	3.50	--
	40-44	3.14	--	--
	45-49	3.06	1.00	2.00
25-29	15-19	--	--	--
	20-24	--	--	--
	25-29	0.33	--	--
	30-34	1.47	--	--
	35-39	2.49	1.43	2.00
	40-44	2.32	2.00	3.00
	45-49	2.72	--	--
30+	15-19	--	--	--
	20-24	--	--	--
	25-29	--	--	--
	30-34	1.13	--	--
	35-39	0.93	1.00	3.00
	40-44	1.64	--	--
	45-49	1.75	--	--

Source: Unpublished 1971 Census Data of Canada

Table 3.15
(continued)

| | Birthplace | | |
Other Asian Countries	Other Commonwealth Countries	Other Countries	Total
0.42	--	--	0.36
1.39	0.33	0.99	1.28
2.64	2.25	1.92	2.45
3.06	--	2.57	2.93
3.54	--	2.40	3.38
5.10	--	2.69	4.11
4.48	--	3.85	4.15
--	--	--	--
0.71	0.50	0.30	0.51
1.48	1.18	1.03	1.35
2.43	1.69	2.10	2.36
3.09	3.50	2.27	2.88
3.36	6.18	2.71	3.20
4.17	4.50	3.00	3.33
--	--	--	--
--	--	--	--
0.54	0.80	0.51	0.52
1.42	1.73	1.27	1.40
2.48	2.50	2.27	2.41
2.90	--	1.78	2.37
3.10	--	2.48	2.74
--	--	--	--
--	--	--	--
--	--	--	--
0.59	0.40	0.58	0.61
1.39	1.55	1.23	1.28
1.52	--	0.73	1.32
2.14	--	1.45	1.78

marriage, the Chinese born in China consistently maintain larger family sizes than their Canadian-born counterparts. But the fertility pattern observed among women born outside China does not seem to conform, once age at marriage and age are controlled. For example, those who were born in the United Kingdom seem to have higher levels of fertility in older age groups but lower at lower age at marriage groups. For other Asians and non-Asian-born Chinese women, though there is a tendency to have higher family sizes compared to the Canadian born, it is not always consistent.

In the case of the Japanese, the original observations made regarding fertility differentials between Canadian and foreign-born women do not seem to be valid after age at marriage and age are controlled. Among the younger marriage cohorts, the Asian-born women in the older age groups seem to preserve lower levels of reproduction in comparison with Canadian-born Japanese women. However, the controls introduced do not seem to make much difference with the East Indian women. Southeast-Asian-born women do have lower levels of reproduction than those born in other countries, who have higher levels of reproduction compared to the Canadian born women.

From past research, it is clear that three conclusions emerge from the analysis of nativity and fertility. Some researchers have indicated in some instances that the lower fertility of the foreign born may be primarily a reflection of differences in social and economic variables (Balakrishnan et al., 1979), and others have implied that cultural factors are the primary determinants (Balakrishnan et al., 1975). Still others have tended to take intermediate positions arguing that both sets of factors are important (Kalbach and McVey, 1979). From our results above, it is possible to argue that, along with compositional differences, the historical factors associated with the ethnic groups are also important in the study of nativity and fertility.

3.4 CONCLUSIONS

In this chapter, we have demonstrated that there are family size differences among Asian ethnic groups. These differences vary by birth order, as was demonstrated by the use of parity progression ratios and the life table approach. The results suggest that the Japanese women are over-represented in the lower birth orders followed by the East Indians and then the Chinese. The opposite is the case at the higher birth orders. It is also noticed that the Japanese ethnic group has a higher number of childless couples.

After establishing the fertility differences, we have made an attempt to identify the sources of variation in family sizes in the absence of compositional control variables. The age structure has an important implication for the fertility differences. For example, the East Indians' lower family sizes may be simply due to their young age structure. The other contributing factor is the truncation bias due to the census date. That is to say the smaller family sizes of the East Indians may be because of a generally shorter duration of marriage.

In order to account for the relative contribution of present age of the woman and age at marriage in explaining family size differences of Asian couples, a technique developed by Page (1977) was employed. Based on this analysis, it may be concluded that age structure is more important than marriage duration among Asian ethnic groups' fertility. However, as marriage duration increased, the fertility also increased for these groups, but it does not seem to contribute to any irregularities in the fertility patterns.

The results based on the analysis of nativity and fertility do not corroborate the earlier findings that foreign place of birth tends to have a negative effect on childbearing. However, we have found that not all foreign-born women have lower fertility than native-born women among Asians. For instance, those who were born in China among Chinese and East Indian immigrants tend to have higher fertility than their native-born counterparts. We conclude that, along with nativity effects, other effects such as differences in characteristics and historical factors may also play important roles in differentiating fertility behaviour. Sociologically, it would be important to decompose the nativity effect so that we may know whether cultural norms are in operation, such that fertility levels are reduced.

It is interesting to note that sometimes the Canadian born females experience lower fertility in relation to the foreign born. This pattern may be a reflection of social psychological insecurities. As couples experience upward mobility, they make sacrifices in family size in order to achieve and maintain expected levels of socio-economic status. This proposition introduces the relevance of the minority group status hypothesis to explain groups' fertility variation. The purpose of next two chapters of this book is to study the applicability of the minority group status hypothesis in the context of Asian ethnic fertility differentials in Canada.

Some possible research considerations to further explore would include the noted nativity effects on fertility. It is possible that cultural norms and/or migration selectivity in terms of characteristics and lower migrant fertility are reflected in the independent effect of nativity (Lee, 1966; Ritchey, 1976). One could investigate these possibilities by comparing the fertility of foreign-born national groups in relation to their Canadian-born counterparts as we did above. The fact that the Canadian born showed different patterns from their foreign-born counterparts indicates that the selectivity hypothesis may be relevant. In case both groups experience similar fertility, one could advance a cultural hypothesis.

4

The Effect of Minority Group Status on Fertility:
A Re-Examination

4.1 INTRODUCTION

Traditionally, fertility differentials between groups or
subpopulations have been correlated with differences in
socio-economic characteristics. Differences in family size
across groups were thought to be a function of variations in
the composition of those groups on variables such as income,
occupation, education, and rural-urban residence. But, even
when differences in these characteristics are eliminated
through equalitarian social change, or statistically through
standardization or some other form of control, the differences
in family size across subpopulations do not disappear. This
has led directly to investigation of the causes and consequences of the observed variation. One of the explanations
for fertility differences among groups is attributed to
cultural traditions. According to Frisbie and Bean (1978),
underlying this perspective is a conceptualization of
subpopulations that parallels rather closely Schermerhorn's
(1970) definition of an ethnic group: "A collectivity within
a larger society having real or putative common ancestry,
memories of a shared historical past, and a cultural focus on
one or more symbolic elements defined as the epitome of
peoplehood." (p. 12) Examples of symbolic elements include
kinship patterns, nationality, language, phenotypical
features, and religious affiliation. For analytical purposes,
this type of explanation is referred to as the "cultural
approach."

An alternative explanation of family size differences
depends upon the extent to which subpopulations have obtained
access to and have been assimilated into the economic and
political structures of the larger society (Frisbie and Bean,
1978). The research in this direction, involving sources of
structural differences (for inequalities), is referred to as
the "structural approach." In general, the underlying assumption (often implicit) is that the subpopulations constitute

minorities, that is, "groups whose members experience a wide range of discriminating behaviour and frequently are relegated to positions low in the status hierarchy." (Gittler, 1956; quoted in Frisbie and Bean, 1978:3)

Frisbie and Bean (1978) rightly point out that an ethnic group may or may not be a minority. That is, maintenance of historic cultural distinctions does not mean that a group will necessarily exercise only a minimal degree of power and resource control. Furthermore, an ethnic group may be a minority at one point in time but not at another. They also make it clear that the two approaches are not necessarily mutually exclusive and certainly not contradictory.

The purpose of this chapter is to review the literature pertaining to the minority-group status hypothesis, which has been used to explain fertility differences between minority and majority populations. This review will illustrate the differences between the above mentioned approaches and the difficulties that beset them, separately and in combination. In the light of critical assessment of past research, an attempt will be made to reconceptualize the minority group status hypothesis.

4.2 REVIEW OF THE LITERATURE: MINORITY STATUS AND FERTILITY

During the last ten to fifteen years, research on ethnicity and fertility has given special attention to the development of the minority group status hypothesis as an alternative to the characteristics-assimilation hypothesis. According to the characteristics-assimilation hypothesis, fertility differentials between groups should disappear when various social, demographic, and economic characteristics are statistically controlled. The alternative proposition indicates that "even when groups are similar socially, demographically, and economically, minority group membership will continue to exert an effect on fertility." (Rindfuss and Sweet, 1977) The systematic formulation and elaboration of these can be found in a well-known article of Goldscheider and Uhlenberg (1969).

Goldscheider and Uhlenberg (1969) made an attempt to assess the adequacy of the characteristics-assimilation hypothesis, focusing on four minority groups in the United States-- blacks, Jews, Japanese Americans, and Catholics--based on previously published studies. After assessing the previous research on religion, ethnicity, and fertility, they came to the conclusion that the characteristics hypothesis is inadequate to explain the fertility differences of the ethnic groups they considered. They found that, in comparison with majority whites, Catholics exhibited higher fertility, whereas Jews, higher status blacks, urban Japanese Americans, and Japanese Americans outside the West region all showed lower fertility. This led them to look for the possibility of an interaction effect between religion, ethnicity, and social organization. This suggested to them the minority group status hypothesis, which does not apply to the Catholic fertility (they argue that the higher Catholic fertility reflects the pronatalist norms of Catholicism). Their minority group status hypothesis applies only to the lower fertility of Jews, higher status blacks, and Japanese Americans. They argue that the social-psychological insecurities of minority group membership operate to depress fertility below majority levels when:

(1) Acculturation of minority group members has occurred in conjunction or with the desire for acculturation
(2) Equalization of social and economic characteristics occurs, particularly in middle and upper social class levels, and/or there is a desire for social and economic mobility
(3) There is no pronatalist ideology associated with the minority group and no norm discouraging the use of efficient contraceptives. (p. 272)

Their assumption in (item 1) is that minority couples are acculturated, that minority couples embrace the norms and values of the larger society, including those pertaining to socio-economic attainment. However, full realization of these goals does not often occur. Hence, minority couples may assimilate on some dimensions (e.g., education or occupation) but not on others (e.g., primary group attachments or intermarriage). The extent to which this discrepancy occurs in different types of assimilation places minority couples in marginal positions, thus producing insecurities with respect to the socio-economic attainment that has occurred. To counteract such feelings and to solidify their socio-economic position, minority couples limit their family sizes. This kind of effect is presumed to operate most strongly among higher status couples who are sufficiently assimilated to experience the feelings of insecurity (see Bean and Marcum, 1978).

Sly (1970) was the first to examine Goldscheider and Uhlenberg's proposition that minority group status has an independent effect on fertility. He compared white and non-white fertility, taking into consideration the socio-economic factors of education, income, and occupation. He analyzed his data using two statistical methods--descriptive statistics (correlation, crosstabs, etc.) and analysis of variance. He found that, when applying descriptive statistics to the data, the minority group status hypothesis was generally supported. However, this was not true when Sly applied a three-way analysis of variance to verify not only the main effect of race but also the interaction of race with characteristics variables to examine Goldscheider and Uhlenberg's argument that minority status exerts an independent effect to lower fertility. Sly's findings suggested that when all the regions of the United States were considered, the minority status effect gained support. But, when the South was deleted from the analysis, the characteristics hypothesis is supported. In other words, in the South, minority status is an important factor which explains fertility differentials between whites and non-whites. Whereas outside the South, the family size differences between the two groups are primarily a function of the characteristics variables. The procedure followed by Sly is the specification of minority status effect as the main effect of race and the interaction effect of race with structural variables (e.g., education) as the "effect due to insecurities." The logic implied here is that the relationship between minority status and fertility does not operate at all socio-economic levels. Equalization of social and economic characteristics at higher socio-economic status may indicate perceived opportunity for social mobility on the part of the minority. Thus, minority group members may consider family size limitation as a means to achieve the goal of social mobility. In this case, the interaction term is expected to be negative. This approach was also adopted by Roberts and Lee (1974), Jiobu and Marshall (1977), and Ritchey (1975). Lopez and Sabagh (1978) went further in explaining the minority status effect in terms of the influence of subcultural factors such as norms about family size.

Roberts and Lee (1974) studied current and cumulative fertility among three classifications of minority status: white-non-white, majority-minority, and Spanish-other-black. Although the results showed that all three classifications supported the minority group status hypothesis, the main effect of the Spanish-other-black classification on current fertility was stronger than that of the other two classifications. The interaction effect of ethnicity and each of the structural factors on current fertility was not found. It should be noted that, while the findings of Roberts and Lee conflict with those of Sly, they do give support to Goldscheider and Uhlenberg's minority group status hypothesis. They further suggest that social-psychological factors should be studied to determine how fertility is affected by ethnicity.

Using the 1970 U.S. public use sample tapes, Ritchey (1975) found that the minority-status hypothesis is supported partially. However, he also suggests:

> ...that with the assimilation of minority groups, the fertility of the majority and minority groups converge. Thus, minority group status is relevant for understanding the current fertility differential between blacks and whites; but at the future point of an assimilated black population, blacks and whites may be expected to have similar fertility. (p. 257)

In their study, Jiobu and Marshall (1977) compared the family size of Chinese, Japanese, and Filipino Americans to native whites using 1970 public use sample tapes for Hawaii and California. They found that minority group status does influence family size. However, the sign of the parameter of the minority -status effect is contradictory to the prediction of the hypothesis of Goldscheider and Uhlenberg. Thus, they rejected the view that minority status will always reduce fertility. They argue that the inter-group differences in values and behaviour persist even when minorities achieve the same socio-economic status as native whites. Thus, their contention is that fertility differentials should be considered as resulting from the interaction between structural and cultural assimilation as well as the history and traditions of particular groups. This controversy was later dealt with by Lopez and Sabagh (1978).

In their study of Los Angeles Chicanos (Americans of Mexican and Southwest hispanic descent), Lopez and Sabagh decomposed the minority status effect into two components: normative and structural effects. They employed correlation and regression analyses. Fertility was measured by the number of live births; control variables included wife's schooling, husband's schooling, husband's occupational status, and wife's age at marriage. Their results show that ethnicity and socio-economic measures are generally negatively correlated. The correlation coefficients (r's) and betas of age at marriage and minority status are negative. The relationship between ethnicity and fertility is weak and positive (r=.11).

An interesting aspect of Lopez and Sabagh's study is their distinction among "social," "media," and "context" ethnicity. Their argument is as follows:

> [A]ny measure of ethnicity as a distinct dimension has to be as uncontaminated as possible by indicators of low status or other general traits associated with having large families. We suggest that having mostly other Chicano friends and using Spanish at home ("social ethnicity") along with watching and listening to Spanish T.V. and radio ("media ethnicity") are the best indicators of sociocultural ethnic integration for Chicanos. (p. 1493)

Their context ethnicity refers to ethnic homogeneity of neighbourhood and husband's fellow workers.

Social and media ethnicity among all younger married couples aged 25 to 34 are negatively correlated with the number of live births (r ranging from -.10 to -.16), while context ethnicity is positively correlated (.32 and .34). However, among United States-raised younger couples, correlations between fertility and social and media ethnicity are insignificant, but, for context ethnicity, the correlation is strong and positive. The pattern remains the same for

Mexican-raised couples except that the correlation between context ethnicity and fertility is about zero. These results are interpreted by Lopez and Sabagh as support for the effects of structural forces such as discrimination and resource deprivation, not subcultural values, to explain the high fertility of Chicanos. This argument, in a way, goes against Goldscheider and Uhlenberg's suggestion that the structural-effects explanation is concerned with why minority persons with lower ethnic integration reveal lower fertility than the majority group (see Marcum, 1980 for a further discussion of this issue). We will deal with this controversy in a later section. Similar to Lopez and Sabagh, Trovato and Burch (1980), in their study of selected ethnic group fertility differences in Canada, suggest that an ethnic -effect may contain two causal sources which affect fertility: (1) Structural effects such as minority group discrimination and social-psychological insecurities associated with marginality (2) the subcultural, or particularized ideology effect regarding minority group's fertility. These two causes, unless they are measured directly, may be confounded in any empirically observed total effect of minority status on fertility. Moreover, the structural and subcultural effects may not, in many cases, be exclusive of each other. This suggests that, in reality, subcultural norms alone or in conjunction with insecurities may account for an ethnic effect on family size (p. 6).

Johnson (1979) examined the minority-status hypothesis by analyzing black and white women surveyed for the 1970 National Fertility Study of the United States. In that study, she decomposed the variance in fertility explained by the inter-action of race and education into five vector contrasts. However, the findings did not support the minority-status hypothesis that highly educated blacks would demonstrate lower fertility than highly educated white couples due to social psychological insecurities. Johnson concludes:

> Racial disparities in average number of children ever born were produced within three educational categories. Black women had borne larger numbers of children on the average than their white peers among those having an elementary school education, as well as among those having dropped out of or having completed high school. Within each level of college attendance, however, no black-white differences in mean fertility were found. These findings thus supported the weak form of the characteristics hypothesis. (pp. 1398-99)

In their recent article, Johnson and Nishida (1980) have compared the fertility of Japanese and Chinese in Hawaii and California, using 1970 public- use sample tapes. Their rationale is that these two states provide a natural exper-iment for testing the minority-status theory of fertility.

The absence of any racial minority in Hawaii suggests that the minority-status hypothesis cannot explain racial differentials for that state. On the other hand, whites are in a large majority in California, where significant concentrations of Japanese and Chinese occur, making the populations of Hawaii and California a natural experiment for testing the minority-status hypothesis of fertility.

The findings of Johnson and Nishida suggest that most of the explained variance in family size can be attributed to socio-economic and demographic factors. Furthermore, no differences in fertility were found among Japanese, Chinese, and whites in Hawaii after controlling for compositional differences. In California, there were also no significant differences among the three groups in their fertility levels. However the Japanese and Chinese had lower fertility in California than in Hawaii. The authors argue that minority status may have depressed the fertility of Japanese and Chinese women in California.

To recapitulate, most studies published in the last decade tended to focus on the verification of the minority group status hypothesis as opposed to the characteristics-assimilation hypothesis. As noted by some researchers (Trovato and Burch, 1980) these two hypotheses are not mutually exclusive, but others stated that a minority status effect may reflect either structural or normative influences (Lopez and Sabagh, 1978). As far as the verification of the minority group status hypothesis, certain conditions must be specified under which the hypothesis is supported (Ritchey, 1975; Jiobu and Marshall, 1977; Kennedy, 1973; Johnson and Nishida, 1980). Others like Sly (1970), Stahura and Stahura (1975; 1979), Lunde (1965), Petersen (1961), and Johnson (1979) have provided support for the characteristics-assimilation hypothesis.

4.3 AN ASSESSMENT OF EARLIER RESEARCH

The review of the literature clearly indicates that there are two distinct hypotheses for explaining family size variations among majority-minority populations: (1) the characteristics or assimilationist hypothesis; and (2) the minority-group status hypothesis. Researchers, however, tend to apply variations in these hypotheses, e.g., "weak form of characteristics" hypothesis, "strong form of characteristics" hypothesis, "weak form of minority group status" hypothesis, and "strong form of minority group status" hypothesis (Sly, 1970; Lopez and Sabagh, 1978; Johnson, 1979). Johnson (1979) considers these variations as four complementary interpretations of majority-minority differences in fertility. She defines these four interpretations in the context of black-white differences in fertility as follows:

The strong form of the characteristics hypothesis argues that once the differences in compositional factors between blacks and whites have been statistically controlled, race will retain no net relationship to number of children born to women at any level of educational achievement. In contrast, the weak form of the characteristics hypothesis posits that if the compositional factors are rendered similar for blacks and whites through social change, the most highly educated will be the first to depart from a radically distinct childbearing pattern. Consequently, in the early phase of social transition, controlling statistically for black-white compositional differences will remove the effect of race on fertility for the highly educated but not for the less educated. Whereas the strong form of the characteristics position predicts no relationship between race and fertility at any educational level, the weak form predicts an interactive relationship among race, fertility, and education.

The strong form of the minority-status hypothesis predicts that a net direct effect of race on fertility will exist at every level of education, although the direction of the effect is thought to vary with that level. On the other hand, the weak form of the minority-status hypothesis argues that minority-group membership is sensitively linked to fertility only for those who have sought and obtained upward mobility (i.e., the educated minority), for it is these who will encounter the barriers to full economic assimilation. Consequently, both forms of the minority-status hypothesis predict an interactive relationship among race, education, and fertility. (pp. 1397-98)

Similar to Johnson (1979), Tan (1981) elaborated on the relationship among race, socio-economic status (SES), and fertility. The several graphs of Tan, which are useful in understanding the possible types of relationships, are presented in Figure 4.1.

Figure 4.1 represents seven possible hypotheses. Each of the figures is labeled accordingly. Figure 4.1a indicates the "strong form" of the minority group status hypothesis. This hypothesis predicts majority and minority differences in fertility at every level of socio-economic status: higher minority than majority fertility when SES is low; lower minority than majority fertility when SES is high. The "weak form" of the minority group status hypothesis predicts that the ethnic minority fertility is lower when socio-economic status is high, but it is equally high for both the majority and the minority at low socio-economic status (Figure 4.1b).

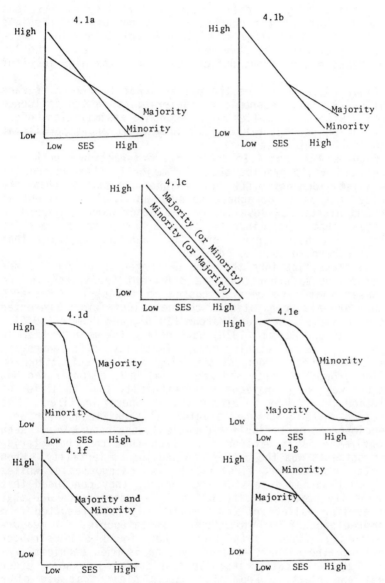

FIG 4.1: Majority-Minority Differences in Fertility by Socioeconomic Status
(SES) (Tan, 1981 : 47)

Similarly, Figure 4.1f and Figure 4.1g represent the "strong" and "weak" forms of the characteristics hypothesis, respectively. The "strong form" of the characteristics perspective would predict no group differences in fertility by SES, but the "weak" form of the characteristics perspective predicts that, in the initial stage of socio-economic transition, there will be higher minority than majority fertility among the low level of SES but no group differences among the high level of SES.

Figure 4.1c indicates the pattern that is likely if race prevails over socio-economic characteristics in its influence on family size. It implies socio-economic assimilation before acculturation so that ethnic fertility differences persist at all socio-economic levels.

Figures 4.1d and 4.1e depict the interaction hypotheses. Figure 4.1d would predict that the majority that adheres to pronatalist ideology will have higher fertility than the minority that does not adhere to such an ideology, except at lower and higher SES levels. On the other hand, Figure 4.1e indicates that the minority that adheres to pronatalist ideology will have higher fertility than the majority that does not adhere to such an ideology.

The classifications that are presented in Figure 4.1 not only help one to understand the different variations in the hypotheses that have been discussed in the earlier research but they are also consistent with the illustrations presented by Johnson (1979), Bean and Marcum (1978), and Chamié (1976).

As Bean and Marcum (1978) have noted, the main problem in interpreting racial-ethnic group fertility differences in terms of minority group status lies in the definition of minority group. Roberts and Lee (1974) have demonstrated how different ways of operationalizing ethnicity lead to different conclusions. When ethnicity, operationalized as "white/non-white," attained statistical significance for only one socio-economic variable (education), the results were seen as confirming Sly's earlier conclusion that the characteristics hypothesis was the better explanation of fertility. When ethnicity was measured first by the two categories of whites and Spanish-surnamed persons and blacks, they concluded that the minority-status hypothesis had been confirmed and that Sly's earlier failure of confirmation may have resulted from the imprecision of his white/non-white categories for measuring minority status. In fact, they found even stronger support for the minority-status hypothesis when ethnicity was measured by three categories: Spanish-surnamed persons, other whites, and blacks. From this it is clear that use of a white-non-white dichotomy to represent majority and minority populations could be misleading, as such a classification ignores culture, physiogamy, and other traits that distinguish racial-ethnic groups (Johnson, 1979).

A further problem in the past research has been how to qualify various subpopulations as minority groups. For some people, minority group is an ethnic group characterized by a small size relative to the total population (Browning, 1975), for others, it is that group which is economically and politically subordinate (Kennedy, 1973). Petersen (1964) defines minority group as: "(i) a historical pattern of opposition from and discrimination by the dominant population; (ii) a relatively clearly defined subculture and separate pattern of social interaction." (p. 237) Wagley and Harris (1959) argue that minority group membership is determined mostly by ascriptive characteristics, such as "socially invented rule of descent", minorities have physical or cultural traits, and there are self-conscious units bound together by the special traits that their members share. In the context of this study, Petersen's definition seems to be a viable one as it covers Goldscheider and Uhlenberg's contentions adequately well.

Goldscheider and Uhlenberg deserve credit for their systematic formulation of the minority group status hypothesis, but it seems that their conceptualization is incomplete and not conclusive. Their minority group status explanation is founded on the assumption that the insecurity and marginality of minority membership are contingent on a desire for social mobility, or maintaining current social status on the part of the minority, and on the potential for accomplishing these. This is at best applicable to upper and upper-middle class blacks in the United States. But it is not clear from their analysis what differences between majority and minority groups occur at lower socio-economic levels, nor the direction such differences would logically take (Ritchey, 1975). If this is the case, according to Figure 4.1, the strong form of the minority group status hypothesis (Figure 4.1a) is not supported. Lopez and Sabagh (1978) rightly argue that the fundamental weakness of Goldscheider and Uhlenberg's study is that they fail to distinguish between what are really two conflicting theories:

> one explaining reduced minority fertility as a reaction to external structural pressures and another explaining high minority fertility in terms of subcultural norms and ideals. With such a two-edged theory it is too easy to account for any minority fertility variation, whether above average or below, both with one consistent theory, not a pair based on theoretically opposed bases. (Lopez and Sabagh, 1978:1492)

Sly (1970) executed a more direct test of the minority group status hypothesis of Goldscheider and Uhlenberg. He based his evidence on a race-education interaction on fertility (higher non-white than white fertility for those having no college exposure, lower non-white than white fertility for those having attended college). Johnson (1979) pointed out that since significant interaction terms involving race were necessary for recognizing a minority status effect on fertility, Sly's use of the statistical technique (analysis of variance) was problematic. While permitting a significance test of the overall race and education interactive term, Sly's study did not provide tests of specific hypotheses relating race and fertility at each educational level. According to Johnson, this limitation was serious because the weak form of the characteristics hypothesis also asserts a significant interactive relationship among race, education, and fertility (Figure 4.1g). This limitation is also applicable to Roberts and Lee (1974), who also used analysis of variance for their study.

Ritchey (1975) challenged Sly's findings and used a regression technique to study minority/majority (black/white) fertility levels using the 1970 census public -use sample tapes. He constructed an aggregate measure of racial inequity for each state based on socio-economic indicators and hypothesized that the race-education interaction would vary directly with the degree of social inequity. He found that the interaction on fertility was strongest for persons living in the high racial-inequity states, but the coefficient was also significant for the fertility of residents in low and medium racial-inequity states.

Unlike Roberts and Lee and Sly, Ritchey did find a pattern similar to the one presented in Figure 4.1a. However, the difference in mean fertility between minority and majority was not consistent across all levels of education. This implies that the multiplicative term represented the composite effect of education on the difference in minority and majority fertility mean values. It should be mentioned that it is possible to have a significant composite effect produced by some but not all educational categories. Since Ritchey did not provide a significance test of the mean difference in fertility of minority and majority at each educational level in his analysis, his study succeeded only in negating the possibility of the noninteractive relationship as in Figure 4.1f (Johnson, 1979).

Johnson (1979) noted the above mentioned methodological limitations and made an attempt to re-examine the relationships among race, socio-economic status, and fertility. Unfortunately, Johnson failed to assess the simultaneous effect of characteristics hypothesis on fertility and the effects of minority group status net of all socio-economic variables. Consequently, she not only rejected the minority-status hypothesis but also predicted the strong form of the characteristics hypothesis (i.e., Figure 4.1f). A year later her own study with Nishida disproved her prediction by supporting the minority-status hypothesis (Johnson and Nishida, 1980).

Bean and Marcum (1978) suggest three factors that may be related to diminished socio-economic distance between minority and majority groups and, thus, that may condition the effect on fertility of minority group status: (1) rural-urban residence, (2) residence in an integrated as opposed to a segregated area, and (3) membership in a generational group that is distant from, rather than proximate to, some place of origin. Use of these concepts would allow one to identify the differential opportunity structures, prevailing in different situations (e.g., urban-rural residence). Moreover, the integrated versus segregated residential areas would indicate the under or over representation of the members of minority groups, which has an important implication for the perception of opportunity structures. If one establishes the evidence regarding prevalence of unequal opportunity structures, it would further strengthen the argument that the theory of relative deprivation becomes an important tool in the study of majority-minority relations.

In the remaining section of this chapter, an attempt will be made to re-conceptualize the theory of minority group status and fertility. On the methodological side, we will emphasize the measurement of the key concepts used in the theory such as cultural integration, structural assimilation, and social-psychological insecurities. It is not enough to examine only the interactive effects of minority status with socio-economic variables as indicators of insecurity effects. The interaction effects are not direct representations of insecurities since group norms and values may be operative in creating the observed statistical interaction effects.

4.4 MINORITY STATUS AND FERTILITY: A RE-CONCEPTUALIZATION

It seems that there is only one hypothesis, namely, whether minority group membership has a net effect on fertility. The so-called characteristics-assimilation hypothesis is just the "null outcome" or lack of support for the original hypothesis (when other characteristics are held constant in multivariate analyses). There are alternative specifications of the hypothesis—an additive model or one that looks at interaction effects (as shown in Figure 4.1). All this would depend upon the theory or social mechanisms that are thought to be at work. Here is where the original theory seems weakest. The idea of psychological insecurity and consequent constraints on fertility in order to mobilize resources for social mobility is a plausible minority group process, but one can think of a variety of other post-hoc interpretations. Since there is no consistent pattern of minority group fertility (across minority groups) relative to the majority, each new study develops a new explanation for the underlying causal dynamics of what is happening. For the social psychological interpretation to be convincing, it would be necessary to measure these attributes directly and model them as intervening variables. The problem is that most studies are based upon data sources without measurements of the key theoretical variables. For this reason, I shall try to re-conceptualize the theory and subsequently suggest how key theoretical variables can be operationalized and specified in a causal system.

The questions that need to be answered are the following: Through which mechanism does minority status act on fertility? How and under what conditions does minority group status alter fertility behaviour? What dimensions of minority group identification affect fertility? Is it possible to revise the theory so that it could explain all minority fertility variation, whether above average or below? A crucial point is whether or not being in a minority group places one in a marginal position within the society resulting in a feeling of insecurity. Even where the "insecurities" explanation has merit, it should be operationalized for empirical verification. In sum, what is required is the direct measurement of key theoretical variables instead of the usual speculation about the meaning of residuals. Hence, what is needed is a revised theory, one that accounts for the dynamics of minority fertility variation, whether above average or below that of the majority. Lopez and Sabagh (1978) came very close to this, but they did not distinguish between the two explanations, one explaining reduced minority fertility and another explaining high minority fertility.

Let us closely examine the argument that external discrimination leads to a smaller family size. Causally, discrimination itself does not produce smaller family sizes, only through some intervening variables. For example, it would make sense to argue that the members of such ethnic groups with perceived low status suffer from feelings of "insecurity"; then one of the "rational" responses to a perceived low status is to lower fertility below what is thought to be the societal norm. This will enable the family to enhance its position in society through social mobility. It is important to note here that the "perceived" minority status and feelings of "insecurity" associated with it are the causes that are deemed to alter fertility behaviour. These are induced by the external discrimination and marginality associated with minority group membership. The ethnic group which qualifies as a minority due to its numerical size need not always be the target of external discrimination; even if it faces discrimination, it need not be translated into depressed fertility. Whether the disadvantaged position of the minority in the society and the insecurities of minority group identification are in fact related to the fertility behaviour and attitudes of the minority should be tested directly. The quality of minority group cohesion and integration becomes a key axis of fertility heterogeneity but not the simple ascriptive characteristic of the ethnic group as a numerical minority. The minority status becomes relevant in fertility explanation only when the distinction between changes in the fertility of minority populations reflects the differential acculturation in conjunction with differential integration and identification with the ethnic group. We therefore argue that ethnicity is a multidimensional concept that cannot be reduced to race, religion, or national origin categories. In Lopez and Sabagh's (1978) words:

> [E]thnicity is not a bag of norms producing auto-matic responses,. . . nor is it a quality one has or lacks. Like any interesting sociological factor, ethnicity is a variable and relative, not reducible to black/white categories. (p. 1496)

Now we are in a position to distinguish between two types of minority populations--those who are conscious of their minority status and those who belong to a minority simply because of numerical size. The former group finds itself in a marginal position by facing the problem of striving for better representation in socio-economic and political sectors, but the latter type is not conscious of its minority status and does not find itself in a conflict with the majority society. The minority which is conscious of its minority status is referred to as the perceived minority, and the one which is not conscious of its status is called an ascribed minority. The more precise definition of an ascribed minority status refers to a group which does not play a distinctive role or pursue its strength of ethnic identity and whose ties neither facilitate nor impede ethnic occupational, residential, and institutional patterns. These people may improve their social and economic position in the society by individual achievement alone and not by participating in social networks that involve mutual obligations and support. On the other hand, perceived minority status involves greater ethnic identity and mainte-nance of intragroup interactions and faith in common beliefs and rituals, kinship networks, group solidarity, and help in the development of specialized institutions such as ethnic clubs, churches, language newspapers, and specialty stores.

The further discussion of ascribed and perceived minority group status goes back to the issue of operationalization of minority group status. Minority group status has been opera-tionalized in the literature at the aggregate level as a subordinate ethnic or racial group. The vagueness of the concept of subordination has resulted in some doubts as to whether it should be conceived as numerical subordination or economic/power subordination. The literature has sometimes emphasized the latter, that is, the socio-economic position of ethnic or racial groups has been used as the determining factor of minority group status, and sometimes the former.

The problem arises when we move from the aggregate categorization of minority group status to the individual or family unit level. Minority status to a large degree depends on ethnic identity, and ethnic identity entails more than just membership. In fact, it can be reasoned that, at the indivi-dual level, ethnic identity involves having a socio-economic status that is similar to that shared by most of its members. As income, education, and occupation become similar to those of the dominant group in the society, the level of ethnic identity tends to decrease. At the aggregate level, the argument has been worded as follows:

> [W]here ethnic alignments rise counter to class alignments, they hinder one kind of social fissure from opening up; where they arise in the same direction, they make the cleavage deeper. (Banton, 1967:337)

Thus, an individual who is a member of an ethnic group categorized as being low in minority group status (e.g., native people in Canada) may have a high income, education, and occupation, thereby reducing his or her level of ethnic identity. It appears as though perceived minority status is a function of socio-economic status. However, it may also be a determinant as well as a consequence. Thus, consideration of the structural milieu is necessary for correctly interpreting and assessing the effects of the individual's attributes on his or her behaviour. For instance, the attribute of being a native Indian--and therefore, possessing minority group status--gains its significance as an independent influence on behaviour to the extent that the social milieu maintains social distance and discriminates on the basis of this attribute.

It may be further argued that the concept of perceived minority group status may also reflect subcultural normative effects. In our earlier discussion, we made it clear that if minority status affects fertility behaviour at all, it is only through some intervening variables. These intervening variables can be studied through the ethnic-culture perspective. The ethnic-culture perspective would allow us to identify differences in beliefs, values, and norms about family size and pattern of living. It is possible that these differences depend upon the context that ethnic minorities are thought of in terms of disadvantaged status (i.e., perceived minority status). This disadvantaged status might have different consequences on distinct cultural groups. For example, those minorities that experience greater economic deprivation and those minorities that are associated with lower social class may resist the assimilation of a "modern" values system and beliefs in the face of perceived minority status. Rather, they are more likely to protect old values of home, family stability, and the national pride. This adherence to a minority culture may result in a lower quality of life. Let us consider people who belong to a group whose educational achievement is below that of the majority. The members have limited access to information through the communication media. This means a slower acquisition of "new" ideas and values and a consequent retention of the old ways of thinking for a longer period than other members. This phenomenon may be reflected in a number of ways such as in attitudes toward the rights of women and how the children should be raised (Grabb, 1982). In most societies, women are less often treated as equals and more likely to be assigned the traditional sex role of wife and mother (Komarovsky, 1964). Children are less likely to be encouraged to be independent and self-reliant and more likely to conform to the wishes of their parents (Kohn, 1969). In short, we want to indicate that a subculture arises in different ways, for example, as a response to the "outside" world (e.g., natives) and as a response to the groups' own needs and traditions in a given situation (e.g., immigrants).

The kind of reasoning discussed above can be extended. The important point is that minorities generally occupy the lower rings of the social class ladder and tend to receive more mutual social support from family and group members resulting in strong family and kinship ties. Nuclear families maintain separate households, but they try to reside close to other kin families. The proximity increases the possibility of support from other family members (Mirowsky and Ross, 1980). Mirowsky and Ross argue that social support decreases stress, and, hence, among lower social class minorities, larger family sizes are rational decisions. They qualify this by stating that not all minorities are alike even if they are of the same social class. Some have high levels of stress; others have low levels. Therefore, they must be differentiated in terms of ethnic culture in order to examine the unconfounded effects of minority status. These qualifications are equally applicable to our earlier discussion of structural effects. The past research has ignored distributional differences between the two populations which affect the fertility differentials while comparing the minority and majority fertility within categories of an independent variable, e.g., education. The point is that structural assimilation varies between communities or areas, and the extent of this assimilation can affect fertility.

In the past, little progress has been made in specifying how minority -group status operates independently to affect fertility. We suggest that to better understand the process, one needs to identify the perception of the minority status by the members of such groups, i.e., the ascribed versus perceived minority status. Once the consciousness of minority status is recognized, we can distinguish between two components of minority status's effect on fertility. These two components are based on the argument that more than one pattern of relationship exists between minority groups and the majority, and fertility depends upon the level of ethnic integration, norms regarding fertility, and type of assimilation taking place. In a sense, this goes against the suggestion of Goldscheider and Uhlenberg (1969) that only one pattern of relationship prevails. In our view, there are two possibilities of minority status influence on fertility: the structural -effects and the normative effects. If structural factors are responsible, higher ethnic integration would lead minority members to have smaller family sizes as an adaptive process. When cultural factors are responsible, higher ethnic integration would lead to larger family size because of greater adherence to the group's pronatalist norms. This is what we refer to as an integrated two-edged theory of minority group status and fertility. This two-edged theory eliminates the fundamental weakness of Goldscheider and Uhlenberg's one-sided theory and is able to account for any minority fertility variation, whether above average or below the majority population.

4.5 ANALYTICAL MODEL OF MINORITY STATUS AND FERTILITY

The development of an analytical model will be useful in the process of operationalization of the model for empirical verification. In an earlier section, we discussed an outline of the revised conceptualization of minority status and fertility theory. According to this outline, if minority status does act on fertility, it does so only through either the structural component or the subcultural normative component. The structural component takes into account behavioural intentions (e.g., to have a child). This views couples as rational beings who seek to maximize utilities and minimize costs (material and psychological) on the basis of individual motivations. Essentially, minority group members will perceive that it is advantageous to strive for small families as one means to promote the likelihood of upward mobility (Ritchey, 1975; Kennedy, 1973). On the other hand, the subcultural-normative component is based on the premise that norms and values favour large families. According to this component, the members of a specific group share ideals and beliefs that differ from those held by the wider society of which they are part (Van Heek, 1956; Burch, 1966; Day, 1968; Ram, 1977). Either of these components produces corresponding effects; the structural component produces the structural effects, and the subcultural normative component produces the subcultural effects. In turn, these effects produce their direct influence on fertility through the social-psychological processes and only indirectly by socio-economic constraints. In other words, the socio-economic determinants are hypothesized to act as exogenous variables either facilitating or constraining social-psychological processes. These social-psychological processes are positioned to be the primary endogenous variables affecting fertility in our model.

Generally speaking, if the re-conceptualized theory of minority status and fertility is to be universally applicable, it must also take into account the environmental factors, situational factors, opportunity structures, mortality levels, means of fertility control, and other intermediate variables. However, the model we are developing is to be applied to the Asian ethnic groups in Canada. In this context, the explicit inclusion of the effect of infant and child mortality and knowledge and use of contraceptives are not included because it is assumed that no significant difference exists between the majority and the minority populations. However, one cannot deny the importance of such factors in fertility studies.

In our proposed model, ethnicity and age are the exogeneous variables. Ethnicity may affect both the structural and subcultural factors. Similarly, age is assumed to affect the other explanatory variables (e.g., characteristics variables). Hence, ethnicity and age may be used as control variables, and their direct and indirect effects on fertility should be examined through the intervening variables. In this model we refer to socio-psychological factors as intervening variables. Examples of such variables are self-esteem, self-concept, and alienation (powerlessness and meaningless). The psychological insecurities associated with these variables, along with the effects of prejudice and discrimination (witnessed by such trends as social distance and occupational segregation), will directly influence the minority persons' behaviour, including their fertility (Li, 1982). It is possible to perceive that minority groups experience social and cultural changes of a different degree at different points in their history. Therefore, the interpretations of minority status effects on fertility must be within a dynamic framework of socio-cultural and historical conditions. The establishment of the socio-cultural and historical context depends on the understanding of the historical background of the groups, along with the use of the already defined concepts of ascribed and perceived minority status. These concepts will measure the quality of minority group cohesion and integration. Researchers have argued that the distinction between changes in the fertility of Irish and Italian Catholics reflects their differential integration and identification with their ethnic group. Minority group cohesion and integration become key axes of fertility heterogeneity within the minority group. In this sense, differentials within subgroups can be interpreted (Goldscheider, 1971).

4.6 OPERATIONALIZATION OF SOME KEY CONCEPTS

Perceived and Ascribed Minority Status

One of the criticisms that we raised regarding previous research on minority group status and fertility is that, for the social psychological interpretation to be convincing, direct measurements of key theoretical variables are needed. Otherwise, it would be impossible to distinguish whether the residual minority fertility left after the socio-economic characteristics have been controlled, is due to cultural differences or due to "structural" factors. Some researchers have argued that residual ethnic differences indicate discrimination, not subcultural variation in values (e.g., Duncan and Duncan, 1968), but others have attributed them to cultural differences (e.g., Roberts and Lee, 1974). Hence, what is needed is the qualitative analysis of ethnic integration and its relationship with fertility. Here, the measurement of the concept of perceived minority group status versus ascribed minority group status may be helpful. It can be argued that ethnic integration is strongly related to the perception of minority status, that is, the higher level of ethnic integration would lead to a stronger perception of minority status. In other words, the indicators of ethnic integration can also help to measure the degree of minority status perception.

Two important indicators of ethnic integration are residential segregation and occupational concentration. In particular, living among members of one's own group places one in the most likely setting for distinctive norms and values to be reinforced (Murguia, 1975; Bean and Marcum, 1978). Hence, it is possible to perceive assimilation of minority- group members as related to residential patterns. Marcum (1980) argues that ethnic integration would be greater in areas where minority- group members are concentrated, since both locations provide the most favourable milieu for intragroup patterns of interaction to develop, which, in turn, work to preserve unique values. In essence, a perception of minority status requires a subsociety, and the latter is not likely to be found in minority households scattered in majority neighbour- hoods. According to Marcum, living in an area of ethnic concentration as well as working with fellow ethnics seems to be a more powerful indicator of within-group patterns of association and, by implication, integration into the minority group's culture.

The existence of perceived minority status assumes that the minority group is being threatened by the majority group. In fact, the minority-group status hypothesis is itself based on this postulate. Residential segregation can imply that the society is divided into hostile groups. The hostile attitude of the majority group toward the minority group generates discrimination against the minority group. This discrimina- tion, in turn, produces the disadvantageous position of the minority group members. The disadvantageous position along with insecurity may produce a perception or consciousness of their minority status. The support for this type of reasoning can also be found in ethnic residential segregation studies. Driedger and Peters (1977) proposed a self-identity hypothesis in this area of inquiry. This hypothesis predicts that the greater the self identity of an ethnic group, the more likely they will be segregated. Balakrishnan (1976; 1982) found support for the social distance hypothesis in Canada. He identifies voluntary and involuntary dimensions for the residential segregation. Within the involuntary dimension, he classifies personal factors and societal or ecological fac- tors. Personal factors include social class affiliation, language facility, and prejudice by the majority. On the other hand, societal or ecological factors consist of indus- trial and occupational structure, ethnic diversity, and size of majority group. Taeuber and Taeuber (1965) found that the case of blacks in the United States was a prime example. They also argue that ethnic residential segregation is basically a function of social distance among ethnic groups, after controlling for socio-economic status. If the social distance hypothesis is supported, the ethnic residential segregation may also become one of the important indicators of prejudice and discrimination.

The reason for choosing ethnic residential segregation as an indicator of the perceived minority status is due mainly to two factors: first, the data required is very straightforward and can be easily obtained from most of the censuses and second, the ready made and well-tested simple index of dissimilarity is available (Balakrishnan, 1976; 1982). The index is the sum of either the positive or negative differences between the proportional distributions of the two ethnic populations. The index ranges from zero to one, indicating complete dissimilarity or similarity between the residential distributions of the two ethnic populations. Balakrishnan (1982) further computes two types of mean indices of segregation; one is the simply arithmetic mean of indices of dissimilarity comprising all possible pairs of ethnic groups. The other is the weighted average of n indices of dissimilarity, one for each ethnic group from all other ethnic groups, where the weights are the proportion of total population in each ethnic group. For our study, we could have as well used Balakrishnan's calculated indices based on 1971 census data, but unfortunately he combined all Asian ethnic groups, which does not suit our purpose.

Another way of measuring the perception of minority status is to study the different determinants of ethnic group formation. In the case of industrialized societies, Hechter (1978) suggests a concept that incorporates each dimension into a new whole: the cultural division of labour. According to him, the cultural division of labour offers a more complex perspective. A cultural division of labour occurs whenever culturally marked groups are distributed in an occupational structure. However, occupational specialization, especially in industrial societies, is always a matter of degree. Other things being equal, an occupationally specialized ethnic group is more likely to develop solidarity than one that is unspecialized (Barth, 1969; Yancey, Ericksen, and Juliani, 1976) because occupations can be an important domain for within-group interaction. Moreover, occupational concentration can be caused by the distribution of opportunities. A study by Granovetter (1974) on patterns of job recruitment among a sample of professional, technical, and managerial workers shows that a major determinant of getting a job depends on an individual's access to relevant networks--through personal contact--which leads to information about where jobs are and how they may be acquired. Laumann (1973) writes that, to the extent that ethnic groups make up friendship networks in given localities, occupational specialization is likely to be enhanced by these processes. Moreover, once an ethnic group attains a monopoly over a relatively valued occupation, incentives are provided for future generations to identify with the group and thereby to resist assimilation (Hechter, 1978). From these arguments, we can safely say that the greater the occupational specialization of a minority group, the higher its resulting solidarity or integrity. Hence, the study of occupational specialization is considered as another indicator of the perceived minority status.

The measurement of occupational specialization is again simple and is used on census data. The required data are the cross classification of ethnicity by occupational categories. The index based on these data, developed by Hechter (1978), measures the extent to which the set of employed persons in such ethnic or cultural group deviates from being randomly distributed among the occupational categories. This is a standardized measure that is insensitive to differences in the size of the cultural groups. The index is defined as follows:

$$X_1 = 10 \sum_{i=1}^{n} \left(\frac{Nij}{Nj} - \frac{1}{K} \right)^2$$

where:

Nij is the number of individuals in the cultural group j employed in occupation i
Nj is the total number of individuals in cultural group j, and K=n=number of occupational categories.

Index of Marginality

The reader may recall that in our discussion of Goldscheider and Uhlenberg on the minority- group status hypothesis, it was mentioned that the psychological insecurity and marginality of minority group membership operate to depress fertility below majority levels because insecurity and marginality are contingent on a desire for social mobility. Further, they argue that minority-majority differences in fertility will continue as long as the two groups share relevant socio-economic attributes at about the same level. Here they imply that structural assimilation and acculturation occur independently.

In this section, we argue that Goldscheider and Uhlenberg either misconceived the notion of assimilation or failed to make it clear. We suggest that the reasonable hypothesis is similar to that of Ritchey (1975):

[I]n the absence of recourse to parallel institutions, structural assimilation of a minority results in its acculturation. If the minority is "absorbed", it ceases to be a minority.

Nevertheless, while the minority is striving for structural assimilation, the independent effects of minority status may operate. (p. 250)

Though we agree with Ritchey, his postulation is incomplete. For a complete understanding of the process of assimilation, we need to distinguish conceptually between structural assimilation and cultural assimilation. To understand these, Gordon's (1978) primary group versus secondary relations are important. In fact, Gordon has a thorough discussion of the nature of assimilation. He argues that the nature of minority group identification assumes that intragroup social contact is fostered, particularly in primary group relations. Such minority groups are high in endogamy, and the close friends and relatives of most minority group members share the same ethnic identity. The interaction between the members of majority and the minority in economic and other "impersonal" spheres of activity do not involve primary group relations in which the shaping of values and norms occur. Thus, even if the minority group gains entrance into the organizational and institutional (formal and informal) sectors of the larger society (i.e., political, economic, and educational) and becomes structurally assimilated, it is not culturally assimilated.

On the other hand, cultural assimilation is nothing but acculturation. The understanding of cultural assimilation can be aided if one distinguishes between two types of cultural patterns and traits: intrinsic and extrinsic. The intrinsic cultural traits include religious beliefs and practises, ethical values, musical tastes, folk recreational patterns, literature, historical language, and a sense of a common past, among others. Some, such as dress, manner, patterns of emotional expression, and the group's adjustment to its local environment, are referred to as extrinsic cultural traits (Gordon, 1978). Complete cultural assimilation refers to an ethnic group's acquisition of the intrinsic and extrinsic traits of the host society.

Now let us examine the relationship between the two types of assimilation processes that we have stated. The study of Gordon (1978) shows that the propositions made by Goldscheider and Uhlenberg (1969) are confusing. Gordon argues that intermarriage is a by-product of structural assimilation. If "marital assimilation" takes place fully, the minority group eventually loses its ethnic identity, and discrimination and insecurity cease to exist. From this, Gordon generalizes as follows: "[O]nce structural assimilation has occurred, either simultaneously with or subsequent to acculturation, all of the other types of assimilation will naturally follow." (p. 178)

Before we start examining measures of marginality, it will be necessary to explain what we mean by marginality. Again, there are two types of marginality: structural marginality and cultural marginality. The "marginal man" is said to be structurally marginal if the group is structurally assimilated at some dimensions but not at all sectors. A member of such a group is characterized by insecurity and the rationality of limiting family size for the sake of social mobility. When the member of a group is faced with choices in behaviour patterns, which reflect differences in the values of the minority group and majority group, then we say that he is marginal culturally. He does not feel fully at home in either group. Though we have made these conceptual distinctions, they probably go together frequently (see Gordon, 1978 for a detailed discussion).

An examination of the measures of marginality requires an in-depth interview to include all aspects of feelings of insecurity and discrimination, intrinsic and extrinsic traits of cultural assimilation, and entrance into cliques, clubs, and institutions of the majority group on a primary group level (i.e., cultural assimilation). Our purpose here is to indicate an index of marginality based primarily on census type data. Moreover our concern is to emphasize the fact that the key theoretical variables in the area of minority status and fertility should be measured for a better understanding of the dynamics of the relationship between minority status and fertility. Even the variables we will use for measuring the index of marginality based on census type data are by no means exhaustive. In sum, we acknowledge that the index of marginality is a rough measure and is not free of error.

It should be mentioned that the index of marginality under discussion refers to a group, and group marginality may be said to exist where most members of a minority group face the problem of adjusting to the values and behaviour patterns (i.e., cultural marginality) or of gaining entrance to some structural organizations (i.e., structural marginality). For the index of marginality, we consider the following variables: marriage styles (intermarriage or intramarriage), language used (the ability to speak one's ethnic language), and social mobility indicators, such as the education of husband and wife, occupational prestige, and family income. Language and intermarriage are taken as indicators of cultural assimilation or acculturation. Price (1963) argues that intermarriage cannot be ignored for the study of ethnic identifications. A high rate of intermarriage results in the group's becoming virtually indistinguishable from the larger society (Beaujot et al., 1982). Similarly, the ability to speak one's ethnic language is the basis on which ethnic groups can retain their distinctiveness. Lieberson (1970) found that language was more important than religion for the resistance of assimilation among ethnic groups in contact. With regard to the variables included as indicators of social mobility, we are assisted in deciding the degree of structural assimilation. There is no need to emphasize the relevance of these variables for a measure of structural assimilation.

4.7 CONCLUSIONS

In this chapter we have presented the review of the literature on the effects of minority status on fertility and also have evaluated the research regarding the minority-status hypothesis as an alternative to the characteristics-assimilation hypothesis. In the evaluation process, we identified the problem of inadequate conceptualization and lack of methodological sophistication in previous research. In the remaining part of the chapter, we tried to re-conceptualize the minority-group status hypothesis as a two-edged theory. According to this, the minority-status hypothesis has two components which affect fertility: structural effects as a reaction to minority group discrimination and social-psychological insecurities associated with marginality, and the subcultural normative effects explaining higher minority fertility in terms of norms and ideals. Moreover, we have also indicated that the test of the minority-group status hypothesis ought to consider identification aspects of "belonging" to a particular group, participation in traditions and activities. For this purpose, we have introduced the concepts of ascribed and perceived minority group status. The measurement of this dimension is based on ethnic neighbourhood formation and cultural division of labour. We hope that these criteria help to determine the extent to which one belongs to a particular ethnic group.

Social-psychological variables such as insecurity or marginality are important aspects of the minority-status hypothesis. It is important to measure these variables directly to evaluate the influence of insecurity on minority fertility. As a rough procedure, we have proposed the measurement of marginality in the context of assimilation and minority group status. Ideally, time-series data are needed to test for assimilation, but we emphasize how the analysis can be improved by the use of census type date.

5
Minority Status and Fertility:
The Canadian Asian Case

In the preceding chapter, we reviewed the literature pertaining to minority status and fertility and restated the various
orientations on the effect of minority group status on family
size. In this chapter, with the aid of this theoretical
reformulation, we propose several hypotheses for empirical
verification with the objective of determining which of the
several patterns depicted in Figure 4.1 emerge in the case of
Asian ethnic groups, using the data from the public use sample
tapes and the special tabulations of the 1971 census of
Canada.

At the very outset, we would like to mention that the
complete testing of the reformulated hypothesis in chapter 4
requires thorough in-depth interviews and/or anthropological
approaches, such as participant observation, to appraise
extensively the subjects' life styles, cultural values, norms,
and beliefs. However, in this chapter, we indicate how one
can measure key concepts of the theory using census data.
This chapter mainly shows the importance of minority status,
if any, among the Chinese and Japanese in Canada.

To test this theory, we require an analysis of the ethnic
fertility differences in relation to some indicators of
socio-economic status when all other demographic factors are
taken into account. In other words, a multivariate analysis
and an examination of interaction effects of socio-economic
status with ethnicity on fertility are needed. Hence, the
special cross-tabulation of 1971 data obtained from Statistics
Canada is not good enough, and we need to use the public use
sample tapes. Unfortunately, the sample tapes do not provide
information on the East Indian ethnic group, as these are
included in the "other Asian" category. Therefore, in this
chapter, we will deal with only the Chinese and Japanese
groups.

Needless to say, the investigation of the minority group
status hypothesis requires the standard population to compare
the fertility of each of the ethnic groups. The standard
group remains as a reference category to check for convergence

in fertility and other aspects of the theory to study each of
the ethnic groups. The standard population, which would act
as the majority group, chosen for this purpose is the British
ethnic group in Canada. This was selected because it constitutes the numerical plurality, and it is the ethnic group that
represents the dominant culture in Canada, the Anglo-Saxon
culture. The choice of the British group as the majority
group is also consistent with other studies (Balakrishnan,
1976; 1982; Trovato and Burch, 1980). Porter (1965) convinc-
ingly argued along these lines regarding the socio-political
issues pertaining to this group's dominant position in Canada.
Porter concluded that, though there are two charter groups in
Canada, the British and the French, the Anglo-Saxons are
dominant and are highly represented at the upper levels of the
social ladder. Clement's (1975) subsequent study which is an
update of Porter's (1965) study, reiterates the position that
Anglophones are still the dominant group in the socio-economic
and political spheres, based on his analysis of concentrated
power and elites in Canada. This adequately justifies our
choice of the British ethnic group as the majority population
in our analysis.

Before we begin with a strategy to assess the effect of
minority status on Oriental fertility in Canada, it is useful
to develop some specific research hypotheses relevant to the
Chinese and the Japanese. The development of these hypotheses
is guided by the theoretical formulation of the minority group
status hypothesis presented in chapter 4. In Figure 4.1,
there are seven diagrammatic presentations of various hypotheses with regard to minority-majority fertility differences
by socio-economic characteristics. In essence, we would like
to see which of the patterns presented in Figure 4.1 will
emerge when the Chinese and the Japanese ethnic differences
are examined in relation to some indicators of socio-economic
status when all other factors influencing fertility are taken
into account.

Research in the area of Oriental fertility behaviour in
the North American context has shown that the Chinese and the
Japanese do not have specific norms or religio-cultural
ideologies encouraging large families. Moreover, there are no
religious, cultural, or social group norms prohibiting the use
of efficient contraceptive methods (Goldscheider, 1971).
Goldscheider has argued that the American Japanese and Chinese
are characterized by higher socio-economic status and are
socially mobile, and hence their fertility levels will be
lower than comparable socio-economic status groups among
native whites. In support of this argument, Jiobu and
Marshall (1977) postulate that historically small families and
the value of quality rather than quantity have been emphasized
in Oriental culture. In the case of Canada, we have seen in
chapter 2 that the Japanese maintain higher levels than the
Chinese on socio-economic characteristics and have also shown
more indications of acculturation than the Chinese. We have
also seen in chapter 3 that Japanese women have smaller family

sizes compared to their Chinese counterparts even after
controlling age and age at marriage. With this background, we
hypothesize that for the Chinese and the Japanese, in the
absence of any established pronatalist norms and given the
tendency to seek socio-economic mobility and acculturation and
the social-psychological insecurities presumably associated
with minority group membership, the effect of minority status
net of any compositional differences is to lower fertility
compared with that of the British majority group. This
hypothesis is expected to gain stronger support among the
Chinese than the Japanese. We also hypothesize that the weak
form of the characteristics thesis will gain support in both
groups. However, we expect this to be more valid among the
Chinese, who maintain lower scores on compositional variables
than the Japanese.

Before we proceed to test the above mentioned hypotheses,
the minority status perspective reformulated in chapter 4
requires the establishment of minority status perception among
the two ethnic groups, along with their marginal position in
the Canadian society. The measurement of ascribed versus
perceived minority status and marginality concepts have been
indicated in chapter 4. Once these concepts are measured and
established using the procedure outlined in chapter 4, we will
begin with the multivariate analysis of Asian ethnic fertility. The findings of the fertility analysis will be discussed
in reference to the specific hypotheses indicated above. The
discussion will also include the relevance of already established concepts such as perceived versus ascribed minority
status and marginality of the Oriental ethnic groups in
Canada. The entire discussion will be in the broader context
of Oriental culture and history.

5.1 MEASUREMENT OF ASCRIBED VERSUS PERCEIVED MINORITY STATUS

In our reformulation of the minority-status hypothesis
and its effects on fertility, the distinction is made between
an ascribed minority group status and a perceived minority
group status, although the two cannot be completely separated.
Once these concepts are measured, we can establish, in the
case of Asian ethnic groups, whether ethnicity is simply an
ascribed trait or a perceived, conscious identity. As we have
already discussed, common heritage need not be an essential
part of ethnicity. What is important for the essential part
of ethnicity is how the sub-populations are organized in terms
of interaction patterns, institutions, personal values,
attitudes, and life-styles (Yancey et al., 1976). This aspect
of ethnicity is useful to the study of social behaviour,
including fertility and family sizes. It is essentially to
capture this dimension of ethnicity that we have introduced
the concepts of ascribed minority status and perceived
minority status.

Due to data limitations, we will use ethnic residential segregation and occupational concentration to distinguish whether the Chinese and the Japanese belong to either the perceived or ascribed minority status. We admit that these are only limited indicators that do not capture the whole dimension of these concepts. However, as we have already argued in the previous chapter, they do have a direct relationship. "The greater the self identity of an ethnic group the more likely they will be segregated." (Balakrishnan 1982:95) Chimbos and Agocs (1983) argue that "residential clusterings involve not only primary attachments of kinship and common place of origin, but also linguistic and cultural familiarity." (Chimbos and Agocs, 1983:17)

Similarly, occupational specialization shows ethnic identity independently of the residential concentrations. "Occupational specialization has a direct link with the primary networks of the ethnic groups." (Anderson and Christie, 1978:28) Chimbos and Agocs (1983) found that the ethnic network gives rise to occupational specialization. In their study of Greek Canadians, they found that minority group support has been an important aspect of moving out of low occupational status simply because members of their group had occupied better jobs and were helpful to the new immigrants.

Chimbos and Agocs (1983) discuss in detail many aspects of residential and occupational concentrations and the ethnic network as support systems in their study of Greek Canadians. In their study, they have shown a pattern or cycle of inter-relationships between residential and occupational concentrations and ethnic support networks. They also indicate the dynamic relationship between occupational specialization and residential concentration as well as their effect on ethnic organization and its institutional development.

Measurement of Residential Segregation

Ethnic residential segregation studies have been invariably confined to urban areas (Lieberson, 1963; Taeuber and Taeuber, 1965; Jones, 1967; Marston, 1969; and Darroch and Marston, 1971). Recent studies in Canada by Balakrishnan (1976; 1982) concerned major metropolitan areas in which there were at least 300 persons in any ethnic group for his 1976 study and at least fifty census tracts in each of the metro-politan areas and a minimum of 500 persons in each of the ethnic groups for his 1982 study. The reasons for such criteria are that very small numbers will not only affect the measure of segregation but will also reduce the validity of the measure due to sampling fluctuations. These reasons are valid for Asian ethnic groups as well.

Based on 1971 census data, we have already observed in Chapter 2 that more than 90 percent of Asian ethnic groups live in urban areas mostly in large metropolitan cities. With this in view, let us first consider the cities with a population of more than 100,000 for the analysis of residential segregation among Asian ethnic groups. It would be useful to consider other major ethnic groups in Canada for the analysis, especially to see wide variations and comparisons. By doing this, we may be in a position to determine whether there is greater segregation among Asians, and if so, what would be the most plausible reason for such segregation. Essentially we want to know whether the residential segregation indices support the "social distance" hypothesis. To examine this hypothesis, we require social distance scales. Unfortunately, we do not have such measures for Canada, but the measures developed for the United States by Bogardus (1928) may be quite useful. According to Bogardus and others, support for the social distance hypothesis is seen if there is greater residential segregation between British and Asian groups than between British and Dutch or between British and any other Western European groups, for example.

Segregation by Ethnicity. Table 5.1 represents residential segregation indices for twenty-two cities with populations of over 100,000 for major Canadian ethnic groups based on the 1971 census data. These cities account for more than 82 percent of the Chinese population and 72 percent of the Japanese in 1971. To give some indication of city sizes, the number of tracts for each city is also presented. The smallest city is Saskatoon with 21 census tracts, and the largest is Montreal with 570 tracts. The last column of the table gives the mean index for each city, which is obtained by computing the mean of the indices of dissimilarity, comprising all possible pairs of ethnic groups; it is the mean of n(n-1)/2 indices of dissimilarity (Balakrishnan, 1982). The interpretation of the last column of Table 5.1 is that inter-city differences exist in mean residential segregation indices. The range is from .735 for Quebec City to .244 for Calgary. The high indices for French cities such as Quebec City and Chicoutimi are obviously due to very high proportions of French and language differences. Another important contribution to such differences could be the size of the city and may not be ethnic diversity (Balakrishnan, 1982). Generally speaking, western Canada maintains lower segregation compared to the eastern regions.

The means of the rows reflect the inter-ethnic variations in segregation. The Chinese and Japanese stand out distinctively as the two most segregated ethnic groups. The opposite of this is true for the British group, followed by Germans and French. This is true for Canada as a whole, as well as for individual cities. We see that with no exception the Chinese and the Japanese are highly segregated for all the twenty-two cities. However, we see pronounced variations within each ethnic group. As Balakrishnan (1982) has pointed out in his study, these variations may be indicative of very small numbers. Considering Chinese and Japanese and their intercity variations, one would get a general impression of

TABLE 5.1

Residential Segregation Indices for the Metropolitan Areas with Population 100,000 and More by Ethnic Groups, Canada, 1971

Metropolitan Area	No. of Tracts	British	French	German	Hungarian	Italian	Dutch	Polish	Russian	Scandinavian	Ukrainian	Chinese	Japanese	Mean* Index for the City
Calgary	77	.227	.237	.218	.277	.378	.266	.236	.311	.222	.220	.387	.462	.244
Chicoutimi	27	.534	.578	.556	.821	.637	.638	.676	.764	.622	.655	.847	NA	.733
Edmonton	88	.280	.303	.293	.334	.477	.314	.294	.343	.273	.291	.424	.587	.321
Halifax	44	.360	.379	.366	.616	.443	.380	.443	.656	.414	.456	.610	.724	.485
Hamilton	109	.312	.330	.324	.336	.426	.444	.388	.489	.378	.338	.570	.488	.382
Kitchener	45	.330	.326	.346	.373	.393	.364	.367	.478	.402	.340	.582	.673	.397
London	59	.300	.303	.300	.344	.390	.384	.338	.456	.352	.352	.581	.618	.372
Montreal	570	.474	.611	.459	.518	.677	.537	.490	.557	.539	.528	.642	.671	.570
Ottawa-Hull	120	.339	.626	.351	.427	.532	.396	.393	.521	.379	.370	.523	.640	.450
Quebec	98	.584	.627	.593	.702	.594	.691	.679	.801	.674	.748	.748	.910	.735
Regina	29	.252	.227	.241	.274	.394	.285	.241	.250	.264	.247	.386	.585	.265
St. Catharines	53	.342	.418	.373	.483	.454	.410	.361	.432	.390	.370	.568	.672	.427
St. Johns NFLD	28	.603	.554	.540	.687	.659	.574	.720	.820	.563	.738	.700	.815	.697
St. Johns NB	43	.438	.454	.472	.640	.509	.482	.644	.764	.464	.631	.680	NA	.618
Saskatoon	21	.247	.267	.245	.260	.406	.266	.251	.302	.255	.251	.393	.743	.289
Sudbury	28	.377	.489	.387	.514	.509	.429	.396	.585	.416	.390	.702	.873	.507
Thunder Bay	25	.306	.311	.304	.420	.343	.474	.306	.406	.304	.307	.596	.569	.365
Toronto	447	.346	.361	.348	.415	.589	.449	.440	.464	.400	.409	.568	.474	.426
Vancouver	179	.285	.294	.278	.323	.446	.329	.276	.298	.277	.264	.530	.430	.303
Victoria	41	.260	.267	.247	.363	.322	.296	.304	.341	.251	.280	.511	.607	.305
Windsor	56	.332	.392	.332	.383	.425	.414	.362	.451	.394	.381	.654	.872	.439
Winnipeg	106	.330	.464	.316	.350	.448	.348	.248	.368	.319	.362	.513	.493	.366
Mean		.357	.401	.359	.448	.475	.417	.407	.494	.389	.406	.578	.645	

*Mean based on all possible pairs of ethnic groups.
Source: Computed from unpublished data from 1971 census of Canada.

the Japanese being more segregated than the Chinese. The population distribution by city indicates that more than 72 percent of the Japanese are concentrated in two cities alone, namely Toronto and Vancouver, while the corresponding proportion of the Chinese population for these cities is around 62 percent. Since very small numbers reduce the validity of the measure due to sampling fluctuations, in order to generalize the relationships of segregation levels in terms of ecological factors such as city size and ethnic diversity, we will consider below only the cities where the Chinese and the Japanese are in substantial numbers.

Segregation and Social Distance. The main objective of this section is to verify the social distance hypothesis based on residential segregation of ethnic groups. On examination of this hypothesis, Balakrishnan (1982) classified ethnic groups broadly in order of increasing social distance from the British as follows: British, Northern and Western European (Scandinavian, German, Dutch, and French); Eastern and Southern European (Polish, Russian, Ukrainian, Hungarian, Italian); and Asiatic. We will use this framework developed by Balakrishnan except that we will consider the Chinese and the Japanese groups separately. Only ten of Canada's largest metropolitan areas were considered: Montreal, Toronto, Ottawa-Hull, Hamilton, London, Windsor, Winnipeg, Edmonton, Calgary, and Vancouver. These metropolitan areas had at least fifty census tracts in 1971 and a minimum of 500 persons in each of the ethnic groups.

In Table 5.2 we represent the mean segregation indices between ethnic groups averaged over the nine metropolitan areas except Montreal, which was excluded because of the language factor which makes the segregation in that city unique. "The very high English-French residential segregation is peculiar to Montreal and its inclusion will distort the patterns prevalent in the other metropolitan areas." (Balakrishnan, 1982:98)

The results of Table 5.2 seem to support the social distance hypothesis. We see that the Japanese and the Chinese have maximum segregation from the charter group, the British. Most of the European groups are closer to the charter group with the exception of the Italians. The Scandinavians and Germans are closest to the charter group. This confirms the earlier findings and supports the social distance hypothesis (Richmond, 1972; Balakrishnan, 1976; 1982). Balakrishnan (1976) argues that the case of the Italians is not justified on the basis of social distance: Segregation may be caused more by socio-economic status and recency of immigration than by social distance.

To further examine the social distance hypothesis, like Balakrishnan (1982), we considered the three large metropolitan areas of Montreal, Toronto, and Calgary. Montreal was selected because of its uniqueness in being predominantly French, Toronto because it is the largest metropolitan area

TABLE 5.2

Mean Segregation Indices of Ethnic Groups (Nine Selected Metropolitan Areas) Canada, 1971

Ethnic Group						Ethnic Groups						
	Chinese	British	French	German	Hungarian	Italian	Dutch	Polish	Russian	Scandinavian	Ukrainian	Japanese
Chinese	-											
British	.496	-										
French	.534	.242	-									
German	.498	.138	.267	-								
Hungarian	.490	.272	.322	.271	-							
Italian	.533	.419	.450	.421	.410	-						
Dutch	.566	.234	.325	.219	.341	.501	-					
Polish	.518	.262	.322	.257	.287	.369	.312	-				
Russian	.559	.347	.404	.344	.370	.479	.400	.347	-			
Scandinavian	.505	.171	.289	.186	.307	.456	.258	.305	.363	-		
Ukrainian	.525	.250	.312	.240	.289	.370	.317	.187	.334	.281	-	
Japanese	.583	.531	.580	.530	.539	.615	.586	.562	.576	.539	.548	-

Source: Computed from unpublished data from 1971 census of Canada.

with a high ethnic diversity, and Calgary because it has the
lowest level of segregation (Balakrishnan, 1982). Tables 5.2
to 5.5 show how the ethnic segregation is independent of the
city type. All the tables show similar patterns of segregation among the ethnic groups discussed above. Indices in
Table 5.2 represent nine metropolitan areas; Table 5.3 shows
Montreal, Table 5.4 Toronto, and Table 5.5 Calgary. Almost
all ethnic groups maintain the lowest segregation indices in
Calgary, followed by Toronto and Montreal. Among all tables,
the Chinese and the Japanese stand out as highly segregated
ethnic groups. We will discuss the relative segregation of
these two groups in the next section.

To have a better picture of the situation, the triangular
matrices for the three cities and for the nine metropolitan
areas together are graphically presented through the use of
smallest space analysis (Lingoes, 1973). The idea behind this
analysis is that it computes a geometric representation of a
data matrix so that the distances between the points (indices
of dissimilarity in our case) represents the ordinal relationships among distances.

In other words, the analysis simplifies the triangular
matrices presented in Tables 5.2 to 5.5 and gives us an
overall picture of segregation patterns. The computer program
used takes the original indices of dissimilarity and converts
them to scalar products. The next step is to factor the
scalar products and reproduce the dissimilarities using only
the first two dimensions and find the monotonic transformation
of the distances which best fits the original dissimilarities
(Lingoes, 1973). These factors have been presented in
Figures 5.1 to 5.4 which correspond to Tables 5.2 to 5.5.

Figure 5.1 demonstrates the pattern of residential
segregation among Canadian ethnic groups. Unlike the Chinese
and the Japanese, the European ethnic groups are closer to the
British charter group. Social distance is greatest between
the charter group and the Chinese and the charter group and
the Japanese. Interestingly, the Chinese and Japanese are not
even close to each other. This reiterates the argument that,
although both are Asian in origin, they possess different
socio-cultural backgrounds. Similarly, among the European -
origin ethnic groups, Italians and Russians are not as closely
associated as the rest of the groups with the British.

Figure 5.2 reflects the uniqueness of Montreal city.
Although Toronto is as big as Montreal, the locations of the
ethnic groups are not comparable. Figure 5.3, for Toronto,
indicates some clustering of Western European ethnic groups
with the exception of Italian and Eastern European ethnic
groups, but the Chinese and the Japanese are farther from the
other ethnic groups. Similar patterns emerge in the case of
Calgary as well (Figure 5.4). The groups that show the
greatest segregation indices are the Japanese and the Chinese.

To summarize, we can conclude that our results confirm
the earlier findings not only of Canadian studies but also of
American studies. These studies have shown that Western and

TABLE 5.3

Mean Segregation Indices of Ethnic Groups: Montreal, 1971

Ethnic Groups

Ethnic Group	Chinese	British	French	German	Hungarian	Italian	Dutch	Polish	Russian	Scandinavian	Ukrainian	Japanese
Chinese	-											
British	.625	-										
French	.749	.545	-									
German	.601	.261	.493	-								
Hungarian	.548	.441	.625	.377	-							
Italian	.763	.668	.560	.642	.683	-						
Dutch	.679	.315	.614	.333	.503	.760	-					
Polish	.571	.408	.517	.401	.438	.571	.524	-				
Russian	.550	.519	.635	.498	.471	.694	.580	.470	-			
Scandinavian	.656	.331	.644	.369	.498	.754	.375	.524	.575	-		
Ukrainian	.654	.455	.538	.455	.525	.576	.559	.311	.496	.564	-	
Japanese	.668	.651	.800	.623	.595	.781	.666	.653	.636	.640	.672	-

Source: Computed from unpublished data from 1971 census of Canada.

TABLE 5.4

Mean Segregation Indices of Ethnic Groups: Toronto, 1971

Ethnic Group	Ethnic Group											
	Chinese	British	French	German	Hungarian	Italian	Dutch	Polish	Russian	Scandinavian	Ukrainian	Japanese
Chinese	-											
British	.532	-										
French	.490	.180	-									
German	.549	.129	.212	-								
Hungarian	.489	.327	.343	.322	-							
Italian	.689	.573	.546	.568	.547	-						
Dutch	.644	.267	.341	.260	.453	.639	-					
Polish	.599	.403	.388	.387	.444	.567	.503	-				
Russian	.572	.421	.421	.411	.431	.611	.519	.401	-			
Scandinavian	.571	.212	.282	.228	.356	.627	.302	.467	.452	-		
Ukrainian	.575	.362	.358	.342	.406	.536	.470	.193	.380	.435	-	
Japanese	.541	.398	.408	.416	.450	.576	.541	.484	.484	.473	.448	-

Source: Computed from unpublished data from 1971 census of Canada.

TABLE 5.5

Mean Segregation Indices of Ethnic Groups: Calgary, 1971

Ethnic Group	Chinese	British	French	German	Hungarian	Italian	Dutch	Polish	Russian	Scandinavian	Ukrainian	Japanese
Chinese	-											
British	.356	-										
French	.372	.124	-									
German	.357	.130	.141	-								
Hungarian	.371	.209	.225	.230	-							
Italian	.408	.368	.375	.322	.361	-						
Dutch	.419	.182	.191	.175	.249	.407	-					
Polish	.357	.173	.178	.154	.188	.311	.215	-				
Russian	.432	.277	.275	.247	.312	.379	.263	.258	-			
Scandinavian	.335	.110	.147	.111	.233	.345	.191	.172·	.261	-		
Ukrainian	.349	.130	.148	.108	.208	.313	.202	.139	.232	.120	-	
Japanese	.506	.434	.431	.425	.461	.574	.429	.448	.490	.418	.470	

Source: Computed from unpublished data from 1971 census of Canada.

FIG 5.1: Smallest Space Analysis, Canada, 1971

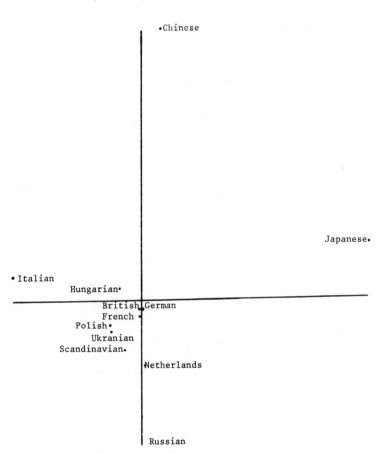

FIG 5.2: Smallest Space Analysis, Montreal, 1971

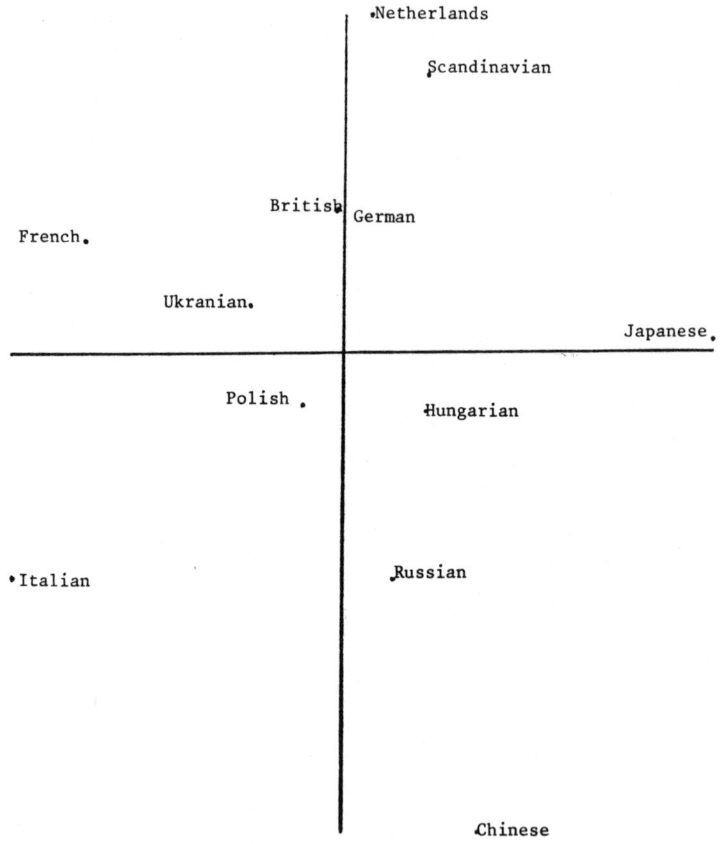

FIG 5.3: Smallest Space Analysis, Toronto, 1971

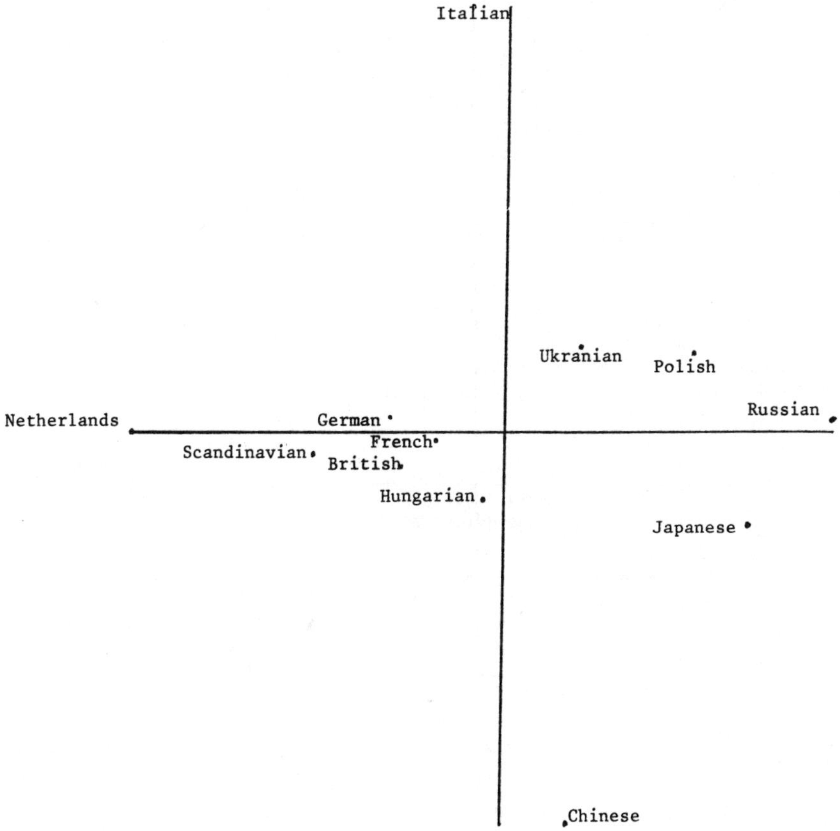

FIG 5.4: Smallest Space Analysis, Calgary, 1971

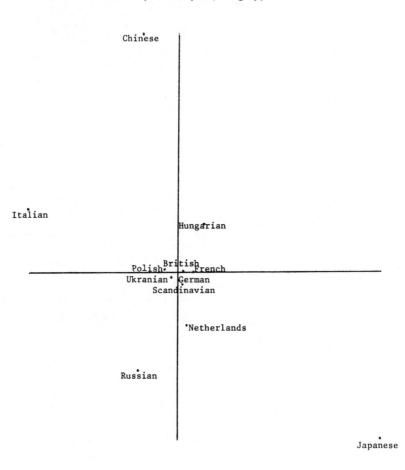

Northern European groups are least segregated among themselves. Eastern Europeans are somewhat more segregated, and Italians and Asiatics are the most segregated (Balakrishnan, 1976; 1982; Guest and Weed, 1976). The reasons offered for such a pattern stem from the social distance hypothesis. The relationship between residential segregation and ethnic cultural background is clear from our analysis. It is possible to perceive that ethnic residential segregation may be transitional and may disappear once the social class differences disappear. It can be also argued that ethnic residential segregation will decrease over time. However, studies have shown that even after controlling for socio-economic status, residential segregation still persists (Balakrishnan, 1982). Consider the case of Japanese immigrants who are mostly second generation or older and are high on socio-economic indicators. The residential segregation for this group can be explained by the greater social distance of this ethnic group from the majority group. Therefore, we may conclude that, at least in the case of the Chinese and Japanese, the social distance hypothesis is valid.

Measurement of Occupational Specialization

To study occupational specialization and its reference to group solidarity, the analysis is confined to males in accordance with previous studies. For example, in his study of Australian immigrants, Lieberson (1963) concentrates on male immigrants. He argues that this is, in itself, standardizing or controlling for differences in the sex ratios of the immigrant groups. In a similar vein, Hechter (1978) confines his analysis of occupational specialization to males in order to eliminate the confounding effects of sex on occupational attainment.

The measure of occupational specialization as defined by Hechter is presented in chapter 4. This measure indicates the extent to which the set of occupied males in each ethnic or cultural group deviates from being randomly distributed among the occupational categories. The index is a standardized measure that is insensitive to differences in the size of the groups under study. In order to see the extent to which some groups specialize in narrowly defined categories, aggregation of discrete occupational categories has to be kept to an absolute minimum (Hechter, 1978). Because of this, though there are as many as 500 subcategories of major occupations, we restrict ourselves to 22 major categories. Moreover, had we considered all the 500 categories, we might have had a problem of empty cells. Another reason for restricting ourselves to 22 categories is the non-availability of detailed data on Asian ethnic groups. The detailed description of these categories and the computational procedure of the measure are presented in Table 5.6.

Table 5.6

Computation of Occupational Specialization Index (X_1) For British, Chinese and Japanese Ethnic Groups, Canada, 1971

Occupational Categories	British		Chinese		Japanese	
	N_{ij}/N_j	$(N_{ij}/N_j-1/K)^2$	N_{ij}/N_j	$(N_{ij}/N_j-1/K)^2$	N_{ij}/N_j	$(N_{ij}/N_j-1/K)^2$
Managerial, Administrative and Related Jobs	0.069	0.000676	0.025	0.000324	0.041	0.000004
Jobs in Natural Sciences, Engineering and Mathematics	0.044	0.000001	0.086	0.001849	0.090	0.002209
Jobs in Social Sciences and Related Fields	0.010	0.001089	0.005	0.001444	0.006	0.001369
Occupations in Religion	0.004	0.001521	0.001	0.001764	0.002	0.001681
Teaching and Related Occupations	0.025	0.000324	0.025	0.000324	0.030	0.000169
Occupations in Medicine and Health	0.014	0.000841	0.036	0.000049	0.021	0.000434
Artistic, Literary, Recreational and Related Occupations	0.011	0.001024	0.009	0.001156	0.015	0.000784
Clerical and Related Occupations	0.086	0.001849	0.066	0.000529	0.070	0.000729
Sales Occupations	0.111	0.004624	0.102	0.003481	0.093	0.0025
Service Occupations	0.090	0.002209	0.363	0.1024	0.075	0.001024
Farming, Horticultural and Animal Husbandry Occupations	0.067	0.000576	0.017	0.000676	0.094	0.002601

Table 5.6
(Continued)

Fishing, Hunting, Trapping and Related Occupations	0.006	0.001369	0.0003	0.0018232	0.000009
Forestry and Logging Occupations	0.009	0.001156	0.002	0.001681	0.001156
Mining and Quarrying Including Oil and Gas Field Occupations	0.009	0.001156	0.001	0.001764	0.001681
Processing Occupations	0.041	0.000004	0.032	0.000121	0.000
Machining and Related Operations	0.034	0.000081	0.012	0.000961	0.000081
Product Fabricating, Assembling and Repairing Occupations	0.077	0.001156	0.043	0.000	0.003844
Construction Trades Occupations	0.086	0.001849	0.016	0.000729	0.0009
Transport Equipment Operating Occupations	0.063	0.0004	0.020	0.000529	0.000484
Materials Handling and Related Occupations	0.031	0.000144	0.021	0.000484	0.000289
Other Crafts and Equipment Operating Occupations	0.020	0.000529	0.007	0.001296	0.000729
Occupations not Elsewhere Classified	0.023	0.0004	0.013	0.0009	0.000676
Occupations not Stated	0.068	0.000625	0.098	0.003025	0.001024
Total		0.023603		0.1273092	0.024377

Source: Unpublished 1971 Census Data of Canada

Before we discuss Table 5.6, it would be useful to mention the two parameters defined by Hechter (1978) regarding the cultural division of labour. These two parameters of the configuration of a cultural division of labour are its degree of hierarchy and degree of segmentation.

A cultural division of labour is hierarchical to the extent that the groups within it (ethnic groups in this case) are differently stratified. A cultural division of labour is segmental to the extent that the ethnic groups within it are occupationally specialized to a high degree. (Hechter, 1978:312)

He realizes that these two factors may be empirically related, but they are analytically independent of each other. He argues that both parameters contribute separately to the strength of ethnic cleavages and corresponding weakness of class as a source of social identity.

If the cultural division of labour is hierarchical, stratification between the ethnic groups will be maximized; on the other hand, if it is segmental, interaction within ethnic groups will be maximized.

Applying the above theory to the Nj/N columns of Table 5.6, which represents the proportional distribution of the ethnic groups by occupations, the division of labour in the case of British ethnic group is characterized by hierarchy. A large proportion of this group is in prestigious occupations such as managerial, administrative, and other white collar jobs including sales, service, and clerical positions. An almost equal proportion of males can be found in low status occupations such as farming, horticulture, animal husbandry, product-fabricating, assembling, repairing, construction, trades, and transport equipment operating occupations. (Please note that we are discussing relative degree between hierarchy and segmentation; we do not have any precise measurements of either hierarchy or segmentation.) However, the discussion of British division of labour as hierarchical, meaning that lower occupational specialization, is supported by the index (X_1^B = .236) (see Hechter, 1978, for a detailed discussion of this issue). Among all the three groups under study, it is the British which shows the lowest occupational concentration compared to the Chinese (X_1^C = 1.273) and the Japanese (X_1^J = .244). The examination of the Nj/N column for the Chinese indicates segmentation. The most preferred occupation for the Chinese is the service category, then sales and the natural sciences. The occupational specialization index of 1.273, compared to the British of .236, implies that the Chinese are more than ten times as specialized in occupations as the British. It is safe to say that the Chinese within-group interaction is considerably higher than the British. This seems to maintain high ethnic identity or solidarity.

The case of the Japanese is not as easy to interpret. Though the occupational specialization index is higher than the British counterpart, it is not significantly different. However, it may be wrong to classify their division of labour as hierarchical because there are extremely low proportions of Japanese in either high or low occupations. Especially in the most prestigious occupations they are least represented. It is difficult to classify their division of labour as either hierarchical or segmental. The possible reasons for this inconclusiveness includes the index itself. It has not been developed well and seems to be quite sensitive to smaller frequencies in different occupational categories. Also, the occupational categories adopted by the Canadian census authorities are too broad. To arrive at some judgment, other relevant factors ought to be considered, namely recency of immigration and discussion of exogamy and endogamy, to assess within-group interaction. The immigration patterns have been different for post-war immigrants. In other words, the group's timing of arrival in addition to cultural differences is an important consideration. Lieberson (1963) argues that temporal variations in immigration coupled with the changing conditions of the receiving society can lead to under-estimating old-new differences. The proposition is that the old groups of immigrants arrived during the period when good farm land was readily available, and the lower proportions of new groups in agricultural pursuits is due to their arrival predominantly in periods after the farming regions were settled. This has relevance to the case of the Japanese immigrants. In chapter 2 we have shown that, unlike either the Chinese or the East Indians, very few Japanese immigrants arrived in the post-war era. Table 5.6 indicates that the Japanese are concentrated in farming and horticulture followed by sales and sciences. Thus there is no clear indication of higher occupational specialization among Japanese. In a later section we will use an index of endogamy, which will indicate that they maintain ethnic solidarity on this measure. We may conclude by saying that, though the Japanese are not as strongly ethnically integrated as the Chinese, they do maintain ethnic solidarity, compared to the British charter group.

In summary, we may say that both Asian ethnic groups, the Chinese and the Japanese, indicate high levels of residential segregation in Canadian metropolitan areas. In addition, the Chinese maintain high occupational specialization. In the context of our study, these results can be interpreted as an indication that these two ethnic groups are highly integrated among themselves and thus they can reinforce subcultural norms. The importance of this segregation is in providing the milieu in which intra-ethnic interactions can occur. We argue that these two minorities in Canada possess perception of their minority status and thus belong to the category of perceived minority status. Residential segregation and occupational concentration reinforce distinctive minority behaviour.

Based on occupational specialization indices, we have concluded that, though both the groups are ethnically internally integrated, the Chinese maintain stronger ethnic solidarity than the Japanese. This conclusion can be further substantiated by the residential segregation indices. The comparison of segregation between the Chinese and the Japanese should be examined based on the indices for Toronto, the largest metropolitan area with the highest ethnic diversity. Moreover, the indices for this city are expected to be stable and more reliable since both these groups have good representation of their respective ethnic origin. The mean segregation indices for this city are presented in Table 5.4. The first column of the table displays the mean indices for the Chinese with respect to the other Canadian ethnic groups in Toronto, and the corresponding figures for the Japanese are found in the last row of the same table. The comparison of the first column with that of the last indicates that the Chinese group maintains higher segregation with each and every ethnic group than the Japanese group. This suggests that the Chinese are likely to possess a higher degree of perception regarding their minority status and maintain better intragroup interactions, kinship networks, and group solidarity than the Japanese.

5.2 MEASUREMENT OF MARGINALITY

As discussed earlier, the concept of marginality is an important aspect of the minority status perspective. When minority and majority groups diverge in fertility behaviour at higher levels of social mobility, it is expressed by the term "marginality" or "insecurity" to denote a socio-psychological state characterized by altered fertility behaviour (Goldscheider and Uhlenberg, 1969). Although many researchers used this concept as an explanation for the differences in fertility between the two groups, none of them makes an attempt to measure it directly. The purpose of this section is to deal with this task.

We distinguished between two types of marginality in chapter 4. This distinction simplifies a complex concept. We referred to the types as cultural marginality and structural marginality. Minority group members may be considered as culturally marginal if they can participate in society's activities and retain an opportunity for the expression of their own cultural interests (Bercovici, 1923). In other words, marginal culture is a mixture of the cultural elements of the subordinate group and of the wider society in which minority group members function. Marginal culture does not depend on geographical but rather on institutional and associational proximity. On the other hand, the marginal man is said to be structurally marginal if he does not confine his secondary group relations and organizational affiliations (i.e., political, economic, and education) to one group. Whether the minority group is either culturally marginal or structurally marginal, the members of the group are character- ized by insecurity. For example, the insecurity associated with structural marginality is expected to produce strong self-consciousness and rationale in behaviour of lower fertil- ity to counteract some of their disadvantages. On the other hand, members of cultural marginality groups often become concerned with group preservation and quantitative strength by following traditional patterns of family life conducive to high fertility.

The procedure of measuring the index of marginality was indicated in chapter 4. The discussion does not include exhaustive combinations of different indicators of cultural and structural assimilation. It is meant to demonstrate a possible way of measuring the index simply based on census - type data. The decision regarding whether the indicators of cultural and structural assimilation maintain higher or lower scores is based on the corresponding indicators of the standard group, the British. In turn, this would help to determine the degree of assimilation or marginal position of the minority group. The members of the minority group are said to be structurally marginal if they are not structurally assimilated completely in the wider society. In a similar way, they can be considered culturally marginal if they are not acculturated completely.

Table 5.7 reveals the status of the Chinese and the Japanese in regard to their position of marginality. Indicators of acculturation considered are marriage patterns and knowledge of their ethnic language. Unfortunately, the 1971 census did not collect data on whether the members of the ethnic group could speak their ethnic language; however, data was collected on the language spoken at home. This was approximated to one's own ethnic language ability. There is yet another limitation in that there were not separate categories of Asian language; instead, they were all included in a residual category. Hence the percentages included in Table 5.7 in connection with ethnic language ability correspond to the percentages of the residual category of the cross table similar to the one presented in Table 2.10. We did not provide any number for the British majority group since one would expect most members of this group speak English. In fact, according to 1971 census data, more than 98 percent of the members speak English. The presentation of this number in Table 5.7 would not make much sense. Simi- larly, we did not complete the last column of Table 5.7 for this ethnic category.

In Table 5.7, we have concluded that the Chinese are neither structurally nor culturally assimilated in the Canadian Society. Indications of acculturation vividly reflect their close network of marriage patterns. More than 90 percent of the Chinese marry in their own ethnic group.

Table 5.7
Measurement of Marginality

Ethnicity	Index of Endogamy	Ability to Speak Ethnic Languages	Family Income						Mean Income	Occupa-tional Prestige
			Less than $5000	$5000-9999	$10000-14999	$15000-19999	$20000-24999	$25000		
British	.45	NA	16%	32%	24%	9%	3%	3%	$8980	High
Chinese	.92	61%	32%	39%	19%	6%	2%	2%	$8335	Low
Japanese	.83	29%	27%	34%	21%	11%	4%	4%	$9733	Median

Level of Education

Ethnicity	Elementary Male Female		Secondary Male Female		Some University Male Female		University Degree Male Female		Degree of Assimilation
British	26%	23%	59%	67%	7%	6%	8%	3%	N/A
Chinese	26%	29%	46%	53%	12%	10%	16%	8%	Moderate Structural Assimilation Low Acculturation
Japanese	18%	20%	57%	64%	10%	9%	15%	8%	High Structural Assimilation Moderate Acculturation

NA - Not Applicable

*Decision based on results of Table 2

Source: Unpublished Data from 1971 Census of Canada

This has serious significance to the marginal culture concept. A pattern of persistent homogamy provides adequate facilities for participation in group life and effectively precludes assimilation in the dominant culture. In case of the Chinese, this point of view is further supported by the members' ability to speak their own language at home. Hence, without any difficulty, the Chinese in Canada can be classified as culturally not assimilated. Regarding structural assimilation at every indicator of social mobility they have lower scores in reference to the British group. Based on their educational level and family income, they may be classified as moderately assimilated at the structural level. This is consistent with our discussion of their historical background characteristics and ethnic integration. The strong ethnic integration and lower socio-economic status aid to classify the Chinese ethnic group as marginal.

The case of the Japanese is not as clear. On some dimensions they seem to have adapted fairly well to their host culture, but on other dimensions they have not. For example, consider the case of their ethnic language ability. Only 29 percent speak their ethnic language at home, and the rest seem to speak English or French. This can be explained partly, if not fully, by their historical background. Most of the Japanese are second- or third-generation immigrants unlike other Asian ethnic groups. The 29 percent who speak their ethnic language probably are those who belong to first-generation immigrants in Canada. Support for this argument can be found in Table 2.10 where we cross classify Asian ethnic groups by language spoken at home controlling for age. Other possible reasons could be that the Japanese are better educated and belong to higher socio-economic backgrounds than their Asian counterparts. Table 5.7 reveals that the Japanese family income is even higher than the British majority group and they are also better educated. Therefore, we label them as highly assimilated at the structural level in Canadian society, at least based on the socio-economic indicators considered in this study.

The Japanese case regarding cultural assimilation has posed a problem for us. We have argued that retention of ethnic language at home has relevance to behavioural (cultural) assimilation. If this is any indication, the Japanese are culturally assimilated. However, cultural assimilation is not supported by the index of endogamy, which is more important than the language indicator. Though we do not rule out the use of one's own ethnic language at home as an indicator of cultural assimilation, it may be only a necessary condition for the purpose but not sufficient. Inevitably, language retention is adversely affected by duration of stay in the host society on the assumption that the longer one has been in the host society, the greater the chances of not retaining one's own ethnic language. Perhaps it is also possible that the longer one has been in the society, the greater the exposure to that culture and the greater chance that one will eventually become assimilated culturally. However, there is no consensus among social scientists, and some have expressed their serious concern regarding the period of immigration as a measure of cultural assimilation in the case of Canada (Richmond and Goldlust, 1974). However, we reason that since most Japanese have been here for two or three generations and that since the number of recent immigrants is negligible compared to other groups, it might be hard for them to retain their ethnic language at home.

The universally accepted indicator of cultural assimilation is intermarriage or homogamy. Interestingly enough, 83 percent of the Japanese still marry within their own ethnic community in spite of the fact that 70 percent of them speak English at home and have been in Canada for more than half a century. Since the index of endogamy is opposed by another indicator of acculturation, the ability to speak ethnic language, we decided to label the Japanese ethnic group in their acculturation level as moderate.

To summarize the results of our review of marginality in view of the proposed specific hypotheses to be tested in the case of the Chinese and the Japanese, both groups tend to be structurally assimilated though to different degrees. Regarding cultural assimilation, the Japanese are more acculturated than the Chinese. The acculturation of Japanese is argued in the context of their socio-economic and historical background characteristics. Most Japanese have been in Canada for two or three generations--approximately 25 percent of the Japanese in Canada are recent immigrants, compared to 75 percent of the Chinese. The Japanese also belong to a high socio-economic status compared to the Chinese because the Chinese do not have equivalent education and occupational skills. In an earlier section, we saw that, though both the groups maintain ethnic solidarity, the Chinese group is more isolated and self-contained and maintains higher ethnic integration. This may be a result of their shorter duration of stay in Canada. In sum, we argue that the differential acculturation of the two groups in conjunction with their differential integration and identification could be due to their different historical and socio-economic factors rather than different religious or particularized ideological norms. The differential family sizes that are observed between the two groups in chapter 3 reflect differential acculturation and integration rather than religious or ideological norms regarding family size and birth control. In order to relate the above established marginality position of the two groups in Canada, consider the effect of nativity on fertility provided in chapter 3. Some of the native-born Oriental women maintain lower family sizes than the foreign born. Interpretation of this phenomenon in the context of minority group status perspective would suggest the following: (1) there seems to be a desire for acculturation, (2) both groups seem to perceive opportunity for social mobility, and (3) we do not have any evidence of any pronatalist ideology or norm discouraging the use of efficient contraceptives. Under these conditions, the established marginal position and the associated insecurities of the two groups are expected to depress fertility below the British majority fertility level. Thus, we conclude that the perception of minority status and marginality position support the proposed minority-status hypothesis indirectly. The direct test of these hypotheses will follow in the subsequent section where multivariate analysis of fertility is developed.

5.3 MULTIVARIATE ANALYSIS OF FERTILITY

In an earlier section of this chapter, we measured the structural integration and ethnic solidarity of the Chinese and Japanese by constructing residential segregation and occupational concentration indices and concluded that both groups belong to the perceived minority status category. In the subsequent section, we discussed the marginal position of the Chinese and Japanese in Canadian society. In reference to the research hypotheses developed in the beginning of this chapter, we argued that perceived minority status, along with the socio-psychological insecurities associated with marginality, tends to depress the fertility of minorities below the majority level. This is in fact taken as an indirect support for the minority-status hypotheses.

In this section, a more direct test of the minority-status hypothesis will be conducted by examining whether the disadvantages and insecurities of minority group identification are in fact related to the fertility behaviour and attitudes of the Chinese and the Japanese group members. This is accomplished by comparing the fertility behaviour of the British majority with the minorities while simultaneously controlling for socio-economic and demographic characteristics. The terms indicating the effect of minority status on fertility are the interaction effects of ethnicity with socio-economic status variables. The logic implied for considering these terms as indicators of minority status effect is discussed in chapter 4.

The basic strategy for testing the proposed specific hypotheses is first to run an additive model followed by an interaction model that includes dummy variable interaction terms relating ethnicity to a given socio-economic status measure. The difference in the amount of variance explained between the interaction and the additive models will be evaluated as to its statistical and substantive significance to see if the particular interaction term in the multivariate equation adds anything significant to the additive model, the one with no interaction terms. The minority group status hypothesis will gain support if the interaction terms are found significant in addition to the increment in explained variance in a multiplicative model compared with an additive one. Otherwise, inspection of the results would be made to verify the characteristics hypothesis.

In addition to the multiplicative model discussed, further sophistication will be introduced in the analysis by using a decomposition technique. This would enable us to evaluate the characteristics and minority group status hypotheses simultaneously. Even if both hypotheses are supported in explaining ethnic fertility differentials by using this procedure, we will be able to ascertain the relative importance of these hypotheses. The detailed description of this technique is described below.

Multiple Regression and Its Decomposition

Multiple regression is probably the most powerful general statistical tool that helps to analyze the relationship between a dependent and a set of independent variables. This technique is used for a variety of purposes such as developing a prediction equation, as a control for other confounding variables, as a description of structural linkages between independent and dependent variables to determine the strength of direct and indirect impact of one variable with the other variables in the path analysis, and as an inferential tool, which involves estimating population parameters from sample observation and hypothesis testing (Kerlinger and Pedhazur, 1973; Tabachnick and Fidell, 1983). However, we will use regression to perform basically a covariates analysis to answer the question whether the minority group status hypothesis is supported or not. In other words, the results of a regression equation involving covariance terms will be compared with an equation excluding such terms. The amount of differences in the results of the two equations would reveal the extent of interaction involved. The creation of these interaction terms in a regression equation will be guided by the theory formulated in chapter 4.

The general form of the regression equation we will use is as follows:

$$Y = b_0 + b_1 X_1 + b_2 X_2 + \ldots + b_n X_n + b_{n+1}(D_1 X_1) + b_{n+2}(D_2 X_1) + b_{n+3}(D_3 X_1) + e$$

where:

b_i is the parameter or regression coefficient for each of the predictors
X_i is the predictor variable (e.g., x_1 = education)
e is the random error term
$i = 1, 2, \ldots, n$
D_1, D_2, and D_3 are dummies for an independent variable, say ethnicity.

The interaction terms $(D_1X_1, D_2X_1,$ and $D_3X_1)$ are created by multiplying D_1 and X_1, by multiplying D_2 and X_1, and by multiplying D_3 and X_1, respectively.

The basic assumptions we are required to make are (1) the relationship between Y and X is linear, (2) the random error terms have zero mean and constant variance (homoscedasticity), and (3) the error terms are uncorrelated so that their covariance is zero for all pairs of different observations. Since our sample size is large, the further assumptions of normal distribution of the dependent variable for a given combination of independent variables may be relaxed.

The method of estimation will be ordinary least squares (OLS) for estimating the parameters. The OLS produces estimators which are unbiased if the assumptions are met, and, even under minor violations of the underlying assumptions, the estimates will be quite robust. The only important restriction in using multiple regression is that the independent variables should not be highly correlated with each other. If they are, the estimated regression coefficients tend to be erroneous and cannot be used to compare the relative contribution of the individual independent variable to the dependent (Kendall, 1976). This problem will be minimized in this study by paring the list of independent variables down to those not highly related with each other by way of examining the correlation matrix.

The results obtained from the regression equation with dummy variables discussed above will be complemented by the application of a regression decompositional model (Coleman et al., 1972). This model will enable us to evaluate the two hypotheses, the characteristics and the minority group status, simultaneously. For instance, the actual differences in average family size (Y_C-Y_A) between the rest of Canada and Asian origin women can be decomposed into the following four components:

$$
\begin{aligned}
(Y_C-Y_A) = \; & 1/2 \sum (bi_C+bi_A)(Xi_C-Xi_A) + & \ldots(A) \\
& 1/2 \sum (bi_C-bi_A)(Si_C+Si_A) + & \ldots(B) \\
& \sum (bo_C-bo_A) + & \ldots(C) \\
& 1/2 \sum (bi_C-bi_A)(Xi_C-Si_C+Xi_A-Si_A) & \ldots(D)
\end{aligned}
$$

The bi are regression coefficients obtained by regressing the dependent variables for each subgroup of population separately, and the Xi and Si refer to the means and standard deviations; bo refers to the intercept in the equations. The subscripts C and A refer to the rest of Canada and Asian-origin group, respectively.

The first component (A) reflects the operationalization of the characteristics hypothesis. It is that portion of the overall decomposition model that determines whether the equalization of the variable means (Xi) weighed by the corresponding average regression coefficients (bi) of the two groups will lead to equalization of fertility by adjusting the observed average fertility of the Asians by the amount derived by this component. The underlying assumption of this method is that the means adequately reflect the compositional differences between the Asian sample and the rest of Canada. If the overall value derived by this component is non-zero, the interpretation is that socio-economic differences do not adequately explain the observed fertility differences. A negative value implies a lowering of family size differences. A zero value indicates that the component A has no effect on either lowering or raising the average family size of the Asians in question.

The next components (B) and (C) represent the interaction effect of ethnicity with the independent variables and the difference between intercepts, respectively. If a value of the interaction component is other than zero (negative or positive), it implies that ethnicity interacts with compositional variables. Inspection of these interaction terms may help us to decide about the nature of the minority status effect on fertility independent of compositional differences. A negative value indicates the net effect of minority status is to lower the fertility of Asians below all other Canadian respondents. On the other hand, a positive value means that the minority couples will have larger family sizes than the rest of the Canadians due to their subcultural norms in favour of pronatalist ideology. In summary, a non-zero difference is interpreted as follows: Even if the two groups have identical means on the various independent variables and even if the net effects of these variables are identical, the family size of the two groups differs by that amount. The sign of the difference would imply which of the two components of the minority-status hypothesis discussed earlier would gain support. The last component (D) is the effect of unmeasured variables. This is the same as the residual term in any regression analysis. The sign of the value of the term would indicate the impact of unmeasured variables on family size of Asians relative to the rest of Canada. No more substantive interpretation is attributed to this term.

Selection of Variables

The selection of variables for a multivariate analysis is restricted by the variables available on the 1 percent sample tapes as the analysis is based primarily on those tapes. The unit of analysis is ever-married females, 15 years or older, classified in accordance with ethnic background. The dependent variable is children ever born. The selection of compositional variables is on the basis of importance attributed by previous studies in Canadian fertility (e.g., Balakrishnan et al., 1979; Beaujot et al., 1982; Henripin, 1972). The selected variables are age of woman, age at first marriage, type of residence in 1971, place of birth, nativity or birthplace, mother tongue, ethnic background, religion, education, family income, labour force participation, and period of immigration. (The justification of these as explanatory variables is discussed in chapter 2.) It is possible that these variables influence fertility behaviour directly and indirectly through other intermediate variables; however, this indirect link is ignored in the analysis since the nature of the census data do not permit analysis (Balakrishnan et al., 1979:148-152).

Some of the variables must be manipulated in order to make them manageable. Completed education is measured by the number of years of formal schooling, and it has been recorded so that it is retained as an interval variable. Labour force participation of the respondent is coded as a dummy variable. A value of 1 is assigned to women who worked before and/or during 1971; those who have never participated in the work force up to the time of the census are assigned a score of 0. Unfortunately, as the data set does not contain any information on the husbands, the occupation and education of the husbands were not included.

As mentioned earlier, the multivariate analysis is based on an individual file of 1 percent public use sample tapes of the 1971 census. It may be mentioned that there are only about 30,000 Chinese and 10,000 Japanese ever-married women according to the 1971 census. This means there would be only 300 Chinese and 100 Japanese women in the 1971 public use sample tapes. As a rule of thumb, we should not have more than ten explanatory variables in the multivariate analysis for meaningful results, especially if we have to make separate analyses of Chinese and Japanese ethnic groups. Because of this limitation, we have to exclude the variables that have many missing values. Inclusion of such variables would reduce the entire sample even further. Hence, the family income variable has been omitted, even though it was important. The respondent's education and labour force participation are the only key variables of socio-economic status. The type of residence was also excluded from the analysis because, as demonstrated in chapter 2, more than 90 percent of Asians reside in urban areas. Similarly, other variables, such as mother tongue and religion, were also excluded from the analysis simply because the religious and mother tongue categories considered in the 1971 census were too general for Asian-origin groups.

One of the hypotheses we are interested in is the assimilation perspective. The operation of this hypothesis in ethnic fertility is often through the generational framework (Beaujot et al., 1982). The idea behind this framework is that fertility behaviour increases over the first three generations. More specifically, Verma (1980) hypothesized that the fertility behaviour of first-generation women would be lowest whereas the native-born women of native-born parents (third generation) would have the highest fertility. Native-born women of foreign-born parents (second generation) are expected to have intermediate fertility. Based on his analysis, Verma (1980) supports these hypotheses in the case of Canadian fertility differentials.

In order to include a generational variable in our analysis, we have constructed a categorical variable which can be considered as a proxy for an assimilation variable. This variable is based on the period of immigration of the respondent and her parents' place of birth. This has four categories, namely ASSIM1 to ASSIM4. The first category refers to the most recent immigrants, those who arrived after 1965. This period has a special significance in Canadian immigration history due to the introduction of the point system in 1967. The second category refers to the first-generation immigrants who arrived in Canada before or during 1965. The third category refers to second-generation women who were born of foreign or mixed parentage. The last category consists of the women who belong to the third generation or more.

Multiple Regression Analysis

The multiple regression equations we use are the ones involving covariance terms and would be compared with those excluding such terms to test the minority status hypothesis. The amount of difference in the explained variance of the dependent variable would indicate the degree of interaction involved. A significant increase in the explained variance due to the interaction term will be taken as support for the minority-status hypothesis. If the hypothesis gains support, the subsequent strategy is to carry out the separate analysis for the Chinese and the Japanese and to test whether the hypothesis gains support in each of the ethnic groups.

In the case of multiple regression with covariance terms, ethnicity is taken as the explanatory variable. Ethnicity has three categories: British, Chinese, and Japanese. Multiple regression requires variables at interval or ratio level of measurement, and thus we constructed dummy terms for nominal variables like ethnicity. Since the dummy variables have arbitrary metric values of 1 and 0, they may be treated as interval variables and inserted into a regression equation. However, the inclusion of all dummies created from a given variable would render the normal equations unsolvable because the nth dummy variable is completely determined by the first n-1 dummies entered into the equation. Hence, it is necessary to exclude one of the dummies from the equation. In fact, the excluded category becomes a reference category by which the effects of the other dummies are evaluated and interpreted. In the present situation, ethnicity has three categories, and we exclude the British ethnic group from the equation to represent that as the reference category. Similarly, the labour force status and assimilation variables are also treated as dummy variables. The never-worked category and ASSIM4 are the reference categories.

In the interaction model, two interaction terms are added to the basic additive model: Ethnicity in a dummy-variable form (being Chinese or Japanese with the British as the omitted category) combined with the socio-economic variable, education. The significance of interaction terms has an immediate bearing on our hypotheses. Education interacting with ethnicity should serve as the socio-economic indicator to test the minority group status hypothesis to see whether the strong form or the weak form holds.

It is possible to find many significant interaction terms which can fit our theoretical framework in a large sample. In fact, one can think of higher order interaction, say, a three-way interaction term, ethnicity by education by family income. However, because of small sample size, we could not introduce such terms due to the fear of many smaller subclasses being empty. On the other hand, inclusion of one interaction term ignores any intercorrelations that might exist among all the relevant interaction terms. Thus, the findings of the analysis discussed in this chapter must be interpreted cautiously.

Before we start interpreting the results of the regression equations, we should indicate how the final sample size was decided for the study. From Table 5.8 it is seen that the total number of cases for the analysis is only 834 in spite of the fact that there are nearly 27,000 ever-married women in the ages 15 and above who belong to the British ethnic group for the purpose of our analysis. Retaining this huge number compared to 300 Chinese and 100 Japanese women would have resulted in biased estimates in favour of the British group. To make the individual ethnic group samples comparable, we decided to choose a subsample of the British group in the range of 400 to 500. Fortunately, there is a procedure in the Statistical Package for Social Sciences based on stratified random sampling which made it convenient to select a specified sample size. Although we had specified a sample size of 450, we could get only a sample of 436 because of internal rounding problems. Thus, our total sample of 834 consists of 436 British, 303 Chinese, and 95 Japanese ever-married women.

Analysis. Table 5.8 displays a comparison of differences between an additive and an interaction model in partial regression coefficients along with their level of significance and the standardized beta coefficients. At the bottom of the table, we have also provided the mean family sizes and the explained variance in the dependent variable for the two models. In addition to this, we have provided a formula for an F-ratio to determine the significance of change in R^2 due to the addition of interaction terms to the additive model (Johnson, 1979).

The key compositional variables, namely age, age at marriage, eduation of respondent, and labour force status are all statistically significant. Their effect on family size is as expected. The positive effect of age implies that, as age increases the family size also increases, but the reverse is true for the other three variables. Their relative importance is reflected in the beta coefficients. In both types of models, age at marriage occupies the prominent place followed by age and labour force status. Other studies have shown beyond doubt that education has shown an inverse relationship with family size (Balakrishnan et al., 1979). If we use conventional levels of significance, we may conclude that education is not important in the explanation of family size differences in the three ethnic groups considered in this study. This goes against the past research in Canada and elsewhere. Before we refute the established relationship between fertility and education, it is important to know that the statistical significance is a function of sample size. In a large sample situation, statistical significance is easy to attain even if the relationship between the dependent and independent variables is weak. Keeping this in mind, we would raise the level of significance because of small sample size. The F-ratios for the variables which are significant around the value of 0.1 may be considered as statistically significant. This type of ad hoc criterion is not unique to our study, and we have encountered it in many studies with even larger sample sizes (Beaujot et al., 1982).

The generation variable is not at all significant even at the 0.1 level of significance. Before we make any evaluation regarding its implications for the characteristics-assimilation hypothesis, it is necessary to recognize the limitations. It is often found that, if the dependent variable is children ever born, no generational differences are found (Uhlenberg, 1973; Gurak, 1980; Jaffe et al., 1980). However, recently Bean et al. (1984) suggested the use of current fertility instead of cumulative fertility as the dependent variable in order to evaluate the effects of generational status on fertility of immigrant groups. Moreover, their research indicated that analysis of generational differences in fertility based on collapsed age cohorts and children ever born would fail to detect the influence of "subcultural" and "assimilationist" forces on the fertility behaviour of Mexicanorigin women. On the other hand, Beaujot et al. (1982) argue that generation is not a particularly good measure of assimilation and

> [W]hen using it in this manner we must assume that assimilation increases with length of residence. Although this is often the case, it is not difficult to find examples of groups maintaining their ethnic boundaries after several generations. Some authors have even proposed that there can be a phenomenon of "third generation revival" (Hansen, 1938). Thus, we would tend to prefer measures of assimilation that require weaker assumptions. (p. 66)

Table 5.8

Multiple Regression of Children Ever Born on Ethnicity and
Characteristics or Assimilation Variables: Additive and
Interaction Models, Canada, 1971

Independent Variables	Additive Model				Interaction Model			
	Slope	Level of Significance for Slope	Beta	Sample Size	Slope	Level of Significance for Slope	Beta	Sample Size
AGE	.031	.000	.251	834	.032	.000	.252	834
AFEPTMAR	-.099	.000	-.254	834	-.099	.000	-.258	834
EDUCAT	-.031	.092	-.064	834	-.059	.060	-.121	834
LFORCE	-.565	.002	-.109	834	-.539	.003	-.104	834
ASSIM1	-.268	.293	-.044	834	-.253	.319	-.042	834
ASSIM2	-.236	.232	-.052	834	-.231	.243	-.051	834
ASSIM3	-.214	.370	-.035	834	-.230	.335	-.037	834
Chinese	.089	.656	.021	834	-.423	.288	-.097	834

Japanese	.382	.125	.058	834	1.200	.071	.182	834
Chinese XEDUCAT	-.-	-.-	-.-	---	.059	.106	.134	834
Japanese XEDUCAT	-.-	-.-	-.-	---	-.077	.191	-.131	834
Intercept	3.101	.000	-.-	---	3.438	.000	-.-	---

Mean Family Size (y)	2.636	2.636
Explained Variance (R²)	.147	.155
Difference in R²		.008

F ratio* = 4.0 is significant at .02 level of significance

*A significance test of the change in R²s due to the addition of variables to the additive model to obtain the interaction model:

$$F = \frac{(RI^2 - RA^2) / (KI - KA)}{(1 - RI^2) / (N - KI - 1)} \qquad d.f. = KI - KA; \ N - KI - 1$$

where RI² = Percent of Variance explained in an interaction model
     RA² = Percent of Variance explained in an additive model
     N   = Total number of cases
     K   = Number of independent variables in the model

The limitations indicated by Bean et al. (1984) are not strictly applicable to our study. First, we are using age as a control variable in a multivariate framework. Second, only 17 percent of the Japanese in Canada are post-war immigrants, and 75 percent of the Japanese are Canadian born. Moreover, the measure of fertility available to us is based on the data set we have. More important, the mean differences in family sizes of the majority and minority groups are very small. The particular interest for us is the causal dynamics to verify the relative importance of the characteristics-assimilation explanation versus the minority group status hypothesis, not to perform the detailed analysis of any single variable. The generation variable is one of the many variables in the operationalization of the characteristics-assimilation hypothesis. The characteristics hypothesis is assessed by comparing the patterns of fertility differences that occur through additive and interaction models. Moreover, comparison of these models is only a preliminary test for examining the relative importance of the characteristics hypothesis versus the minority group status hypothesis. The confirmative test of the two hypotheses is based on simultaneous evaluation of the explanations of fertility using the regression decomposition technique.

The ethnic effect on fertility based on an additive model is weak and insignificant especially for the Chinese. The precise interpretation of the regression coefficient for the Chinese group is made in reference to the omitted category, the British. In other words, the Chinese group is not significantly different from the British, the charter group. On the other hand, the Japanese group is significantly different from the British group at the 0.1 level. The corresponding terms in an interaction model strongly reiterate our contention by reducing the level of significance for the Japanese from 0.125 to 0.071. This finding will be discussed in the last section of this chapter.

The most intriguing aspect of the ethnic effect on fertility emerges from inspection of interaction effects. Though the independent effect of Chinese ethnic group affiliation is not significantly different from the British, the effect of interaction between the Chinese and their education is significantly different from the effect of the interaction between the British and their education. The corresponding term for the Japanese surprises most, as it is closer to being insignificant. The possible reasons for the differences in interaction terms will be discussed in the final section of this chapter.

In dummy variable regression, the slope of children ever born on education for the British (the omitted category) is simply the coefficient for the variable education (-0.059). The slope for the Chinese is the sum of the coefficients for education and for the interaction term, Chinese X education (-.059 + .059 = .000). Similarly, the slope for the Japanese is the sum of the coefficients for education and the interaction term, Japanese X education (-.059 - .077 = -.136). Clearly, the slopes of children ever born on education for the British (-.059) and the Japanese (-.136) are substantially more negative than for the Chinese (.000) (see Neter and Wasserman, 1974). The zero slope for the Chinese indicates that education has no effect on children ever born for the Chinese when holding constant all other factors. In terms of our hypotheses, however, the result offers an important observation: Education is inversely related to fertility for the Japanese and the British women but has virtually no association with fertility for Chinese women, holding constant other predictor socio-economic and demographic variables. The significant finding in an interaction model is that the inclusion of interaction terms has produced significant changes in R^2, thereby implying that the two interaction terms are important in explaining family size variation.

From our results, we conclude that the significant fertility variation is explicable in part by the interaction terms. It was found that, though the independent effects of ethnicity and education were not significant in the case of the Chinese minority compared to the British majority, the interaction effect of education and the Chinese ethnic background was significantly different from the corresponding term for the British. Concerning the minority status framework, adopted by this analysis, the evidence suggests that "insecurities" do in fact influence reproductive behaviour of the Chinese. In other words, when the majority (the British) and the minority (the Chinese) are made similar on demographic and socio-economic factors, the Chinese ethnic background does not exert an independent effect on fertility for the non-schooled, but its effect on fertility for the schooled is significant. In general terms, disadvantaged Chinese in Canada have higher fertility than the relatively advantaged British at the lower educational level but not so at the higher educational level. The members of the Chinese ethnic group on an average have at least three years less schooling with also larger variation among themselves. It seems possible that, for the majority of the lower educated Chinese, there has been a denial of the opportunity for social mobility, equalization of socio-economic and demographic attributes through greater structural assimilation, and integration of the minority into the socio-economic institutions.

The case of the Japanese is different from the Chinese. The Japanese ethnic background per se affects childbearing and indicates that Japanese women are significantly different from their British counterparts. However, the interaction effect of education and Japanese ethnic background is weak and can hardly be considered as statistically significant. To make any definitive statements concerning the minority-status hypothesis in the case of Japanese fertility behaviour, we need further analysis to dissect the possible factors that may be reflected in the independent effects of ethnicity and its interaction with education to determine the socio-psycho-logical and social structural dimensions associated with the fertility behaviour of Japanese women in Canada.

Based on the above analysis, if we have to come to a conclusion about the minority status framework adopted by this study, we can say with confidence that the minority-status hypothesis is strongly supported in case of the Chinese. Since the Japanese ethnic background also shows significant importance, along with the weaker effect of interaction between ethnicity and education as predictors of fertility, we take this as weak support for the minority group status hypothesis.

Regression Decomposition Analysis. The conclusions drawn in the above paragraph can be considered tentative, and a critical test of the hypotheses can be made by replicating the same analysis for the three ethnic groups separately. The direct comparison of the regression coefficients of the variables and the differences in family sizes decomposition in terms of the produced hypotheses would be a more confirmative test. It would also help us to compare the family size differences of the three groups and the importance of each independent variable in explaining family size variation.

Analogous to Table 5.8, which presents regression and beta coefficients, Table 5.9 presents the results of multiple regression for the three ethnic groups separately. An additional datum in this table is the simple correlation coefficient from which we would know the strength of the relationship between the dependent variable and the predictor variables. The British ethnic group possesses a large sample size compared to the other two because of availability. As the separate regression equations were used for all three groups, there was no need to select a special subsample for the British as there was in Table 5.8.

Immediately, one can see the effect of the large sample size in the case of the British. All the categories of assimilation variable are highly statistically significant indicating that generation is an important variable in explaining fertility behaviour. However, the correlation coefficients make it clear that the relationship between the categories of generation variable and children ever born is not strong. Though all the variables included in the model are highly significant in the case of the British majority group, the explained variation in the dependent variable is still only 16 percent.

The Chinese picture supports our argument made earlier that the educational attainment per se does not influence the Chinese women's attitude toward childbearing. However, their work-status does bring direct bearing on their fertility behaviour. Just being educated is not enough, but whether one works or not is important. Those who take part in the labour force tend to have smaller families. Interestingly, the complete opposite is the case for Japanese women. It is difficult if not impossible to come up with a possible explanation for such contrasting observations. Among other things, we tend to think that historical factors may help us to understand the different attitudes of the Japanese and the Chinese women toward childbearing. Historical factors are not restricted to these groups' history in Canada but their historical background in their respective home countries as well.

Though it is well documented in the literature that female labour force participation is highly correlated with fertility, Ahdab-Yehia (1977:173) has shown that the relationship is not that simple. He argues that women working at or near home (in agriculture, handicrafts, or domestic service) have family sizes very similar to non-working women. What is more important about labour force status and its effect on fertility is the extent to which it involves a real extension of roles beyond the family and into the economic and political realm (Birdsall, 1976). Cheng (1931) documents that most of the Japanese who immigrated prior to World War II were agriculturists, including farmers, landowners, farm labourers, and fishermen. The women who belong to this class help their family on their own farms or work as female help for wages. Hence, it is possible to hypothesize that the Japanese women might have participated in traditional occupations, which may not have had consequences on their fertility behaviour.

Shibata (1980) reports that Japanese women also worked in many other occupations. According to her, lack of education was not at all the problem. Physical strength was the most essential requirement. This was abundant among these women as they had worked hard on farms in Japan before immigrating. Here in Canada

> [T]hey all worked; some as cooks at the logging camps and mining camps, some in canneries or as houseworkers, or small corner store keepers. Their social environment forced them to work. They simply could not stay at home as housewives. Their labour was also necessary to maintain their life in Canada. Compared to Japanese women in Japan, they were more open and liberated due to their socio-economic involvement. They did not have mothers-in-law to work under, as is traditional in Japan. (Shibata, 1980: 262).

On the other hand, Chinese women are very traditional. In chapter 2 we mentioned that most of the Chinese who immigrated before World War II were single men. The Chinese life centres around family. The responsibility of a wife is to look after the family, and she is the centre of the domestic life (Cheng, 1931). It is not the practice of the housewife to work outside the house. In sum, it is possible to perceive that working outside the house is an accepted norm among the

Table 5.9

Multiple Regression of Children Ever Born on
Characteristics or Assimilation Variables by Ethnicity, Canada, 1971

Independent Variables	British					Chinese				
	Slope	Level of Significance for Slope	Beta	Corr Coeff with Dept. Variable (R)	Sample Size	Slope	Level of Significance for Slope	Beta	Corr Coeff with Dept. Variable (R)	Sample Size
AGE	.033	.000	.268	.199	26685	.028	.001	.221	.235	303
AFEFTMAR	-.122	.000	-.295	-.211	26685	-.070	.000	-.233	-.221	303
EDUCAT	-.075	.000	-.104	-.226	26685	.001	.968	.003	-.197	303
LFORCE	-.543	.000	-.100	-.187	26685	-.646	.013	-.143	-.227	303
ASSIM1	-.324	.000	-.022	-.057	26685	.160	.682	.037	-.048	303
ASSIM2	-.369	.000	-.064	-.011	26685	.451	.228	.113	.129	303
ASSIM3	-.103	.000	-.015	.022	26685	-.163	.766	-.020	-.081	303
Intercept	3.817	.000			26685	1.860	.010			303
Mean Family Size (y)	2.564					2.630				
Explained Variance (R²)	.158					.147				

Japanese

Independent Variables	Slope	Level of Significance for Slope	Beta	Corr Coeff with Dept Variable (R)	Sample Size
AGE	.051	.001	.366	.438	95
AGEFTMAR	-.149	.000	-.366	-.335	95
EDUCAT	-.124	.015	-.255	-.410	95
LFORCE	-.121	.786	-.025	-.167	95
ASSIM1	.362	.600	.056	-.096	95
ASSIM2	-.177	.777	-.041	.052	95
ASSIM3	.833	.104	.219	.195	95
Intercept	4.689	.002			95

Mean Family Size (y) 2.674

Explained Variance (R²) .427

Japanese women, but the opposite seems to be the case for Chinese women. If this is the situation, the working wives of Chinese origin should be modern in their attitude, and the associated social contact with Canadian culture is a source of change. This brings the perception of social mobility and the smaller family norm. However, mere labour force participation among Japanese women did not change their attitude toward family limitation. The most important factor for family limitation among Japanese women is education. It is as important as age and age at marriage.

The most distinguishing feature of the Japanese model is that the explained variance in the dependent variable is as high as 43 percent. We can see from the beta values that age, age at marriage, and education are responsible for such a high R^2. It can also be noticed that the assimilation variable category, ASSIM3, is significant indicating that second-generation Japanese women with foreign-born parents have more children than their counterparts with native born-parents.

Table 5.10 utilizes the metric coefficients along with the intercepts from Table 5.9. Means and their corresponding standard deviations are taken from the regression equation computer output to decompose the observed fertility differences between the majority and the minority groups. Components (A) and (B) in the table suggest that the characteristics-assimilation hypothesis as well as the minority status hypothesis, respectively, are important in explaining the differential in family size if the magnitude for these components is significantly different from zero. In such a case, we may say that the two hypotheses are not mutually exclusive but rather are complementary to each other.

Consider the case of the Chinese ethnic group; the subtotal for component (A) has the value of -0.146 which indicates that there would be a fertility reduction of 0.146 child for Chinese women if their variable levels (characteristics) are equalized to the means of British women. The effects of individual variables in the decomposition analysis are as expected. The most striking variable is education. The equalization of Chinese women's educational level to that of British alone produce a 0.103 decrease in fertility of the Chinese.

The minority-status hypothesis is operationalized as the interaction between ethnicity and compositional variables, component (B). The results are quite supportive of this explanation. The direction of the effect is as expected. In comparison to the British majority, the independent effect of minority status of the Chinese serves to reduce fertility by more than one child. This difference is substantial in the context of average family size. The fact that the minority status acts in such a way and in such a magnitude to promote lower fertility of the Chinese is a significant finding. In fact, the magnitude of the interaction effect of education with Chinese ethnic background is surprisingly large. This interaction is of great theoretical interest to us since it

TABLE 5.10

Regression Decomposition of Fertility between Ever-Married British
Women against Chinese and Japanese Women, Canada, 1971

Actual Difference in Family Sizes (British Majority - Oriental Minority)	Chinese -0.066	Japanese -0.110
Variable Levels (A) (Compositional Differences or Assimilation)		
AGE	.092	.031
AGEFTMAR	- .070	.171
EDUCAT	- .103	.025
LFORCE	- .069	- .012
ASSIM 1	.024	- .001
ASSIM 2	- .014	.026
ASSIM 3	- .006	- .145
Subtotal	- .146	.095
Differences between Intercepts (C)	1.957	- .872
Variable Effects (B) (Interaction: Ethnicity with Variables)		
AGE	.079	- .280
AGEFTMAR	- .253	.191
EDUCAT	- .315	.169
LFORCE	- .041	.159
ASSIM 1	- .149	- .153
ASSIM 2	- .359	- .078
ASSIM 3	.017	- .380
Subtotal	-1.021	- .372
Unmeasured (D)	- .856	1.039
TOTAL	-0.066	-0.110

provides unequivocal support for the minority status-hypo-
thesis in the case of Chinese fertility behaviour. The
comparison of the relative magnitudes of components (A) and
(B) sharply questions the notion of omitting minority status
as an explanatory variable in the study of ethnic fertility
differentials.

The results for the Japanese differ from the Chinese but
nevertheless are interesting. The low value of a subtotal for
component (A) for the Japanese may be taken as little or no
support for the characteristics hypothesis. This is possible
due to the fact that there are no differences in socio-economic variables between the Japanese and the British. The
average education for the British women is 10.09 years of
schooling with 3.00 years as standard deviation; the corresponding figures for the Japanese are 10.354 and 3.95 years.
The average family income for the Japanese group is already
higher than the British group. It seems that merely raising
the educational level or the family income is not going to
make much difference in bringing down the Japanese fertility
to the level of the British, unless the corresponding changes
occur in more qualitative dimensions of socio-economic status
such as power, prestige, and political control. This argument
makes sense because, unlike the characteristics hypothesis,
the minority-status hypothesis is supported by the relative
magnitude of component (B) compared to (A). The negative sign
indicates that socio-psychological insecurities associated
with minority status bring down the family size of the
Japanese.

Before we begin the discussion regarding the possible
mechanism of the minority group status hypothesis being
supported from our findings, it would be useful to make some
comments in connection with the actual mean differences in
family sizes of the majority and minority groups. As
presented in Table 5.10, the differences are very small,
particularly between the British and the Chinese. It is
possible that the differences may not be statistically
significant. The question arises whether these differences
are good enough to test the underlying theory using multiple
regression when we know for sure that there is practically
nothing to explain in the differences. The answer for this
question is given in the following paragraph.

In arguing for the merit of the theory in this context,
we must recall that the mean family size differences presented
in Table 5.10 are "zero order" differences computed without
controls. Marshall and Jiobu (1980) argue that, even if the
groups have identical family sizes, it may be for different
reasons. The causal dynamics explaining the means need not be
the same. The decomposition procedure used permits us to
evalute simultaneously different possible explanations.
Though the difference between the British and the Chinese is
as small as 0.066, the difference due to minority status alone
is 1.021. This suggests that, if other factors affecting the
British and the Chinese did not offset the effect of minority

status, the Chinese families would be more than one person smaller than the British families, which is quite significant. The inherent interest is in this factor because of its theoretical importance but not in the "zero-order" difference of mean family sizes of the two groups.

5.4 DISCUSSION AND CONCLUSIONS

The aim of this chapter was to test whether the minority group status hypothesis has any relevance in the case of Oriental ethnic groups in Canada. It may be emphasized that the purpose is to go beyond the study of differential fertility since the relative causal importance of structural and cultural factors is relevant to social demography. To this end, we first measured perceived versus ascribed minority status through occupational and residential segregation which tapped involvement in a distinctive ethnic subculture. This was followed by construction of a marginality index intended to indicate the relative importance of explaining both reduced minority fertility as a reaction to perceived social mobility and high minority fertility in terms of subcultural norms. These explanations are in effect components of the two-edged theory of minority group status outlined in chapter 4. Finally, we examined the patterns of fertility differences that occur through additive and interaction models. Comparison of these models helped us to make a preliminary test for the minority group status hypothesis. As a continuation, we ran separate regression equations for each ethnic group and used regression decomposition techniques to evaluate simultaneously the minority group status and the characteristics hypotheses which are thought to be alternatives to each other.

Now, let us put the findings of Tables 5.9 and 5.10, which support the minority-status hypothesis, into the theoretical perspective discussed in chapter 4. The concepts introduced in the theory, ascribed versus perceived minority status were measured in this chapter, and we concluded that both the groups do retain their distinctiveness, as reflected in their social distance hypothesis in the context of neighbourhood formation and cultural division of labour measured through the occupational specialization index. Though both the groups show strong identification with their ethnic background, it seems that the Chinese exhibit extreme forms of the behaviour which is typical of their group. We mean to imply that the Chinese minority in Canada feel rather strongly about their minority group status compared to the Japanese. This is also justified by the fact that the Chinese fall into the less assimilated category shown by our analysis.

Minority group status consciousness, associated with marginality and insecurity, is expected to affect fertility behaviour. The degree of marginality and, in turn, its effect on fertility behaviour depend on the combinations of assimilation (i.e., cultural assimilation and structural assimilation) taking place. We argue that those couples who are highly assimilated structurally, but are low in acculturation, will have the lowest fertility. The underlying assumption here is that these couples experience the greatest degree of "insecurity" since they are upwardly mobile but are not culturally assimilated. These persons are the ones most likely to adopt the rationality of reducing their fertility for the sake of social mobility. These arguments are consistent with the theory discussed in chapter 4 and as well as with other studies (Trovato, 1978).

Based on the results presented in Table 5.7, we concluded that the Chinese group is low on both cultural and structural assimilation. However, the Japanese differ from the Chinese to the extent that they are high on structural assimilation but moderate on acculturation. These conclusions are consistent with the theme that ethnic groups' differential socio-economic achievement is explained in terms of the cultural adaptability of ethnic minorities in their competition with the dominant group (Wagley and Harris, 1959). It is also possible that other factors such as history played an important role for the Japanese and the Chinese entering different occupations. Li (1979), using an historical approach to the Chinese, has shown that this group's concentration in the service industry, such as laundrymen and restaurant workers, was largely the result of restricted opportunities in the non-ethnic sector.

We have already concluded that the minority group status hypothesis gained strong support among the Chinese and moderate support among the Japanese. After accounting for compositional differences, the Chinese group, which is lower on both structural and cultural assimilation, showed the largest reduction in family size (1.02). On the other hand, the Japanese who are structurally highly assimilated and moderately acculturated, showed reduction in family size of 0.40 child. This result corresponds to the argument of the above paragraphs.

Let us translate the implications of Table 5.7 in view of the minority group status hypothesis being investigated. In other words, what aspect of the theory, the subcultural normative component or the structural component, gains relative importance? Needless to say, the structural forces are analogous to discrimination and resource deprivation which best explain reduction in Oriental minority group fertility in Canada. The evidence we have is more definite than the usual situation where indirect measurement via residuals is done. Both the minorities seem to perceive social mobility as limited by minority status, and hence they consciously limit their fertility in order to actualize their goal. This seems to be possible without both being completely acculturated in the dominant society. Given the Canadian situation of multiculturalism, cultural plurality is a persisting characteristic of Canadian society (Porter, 1965). It is also argued that the cultural differences may change over time to facilitate socio-economic mobility without necessarily eradicating key cultural traditions and psychological traits which define a distinct ethnic identity (Jiobu and Marshall, 1977). Schooler (1976) has shown that some of these key persisting traits could be dysfunctional, based on his analysis of the persisting influence of serfdom on several American ethnic groups. Since only 17 percent of the Japanese group are post-war immigrants and 75 percent of the Japanese are Canadian born, it would be difficult to expect further immediate acculturation of this group, given the nature of the state policy.

The question that has not been answered so far is why the minority group status hypothesis did not gain strong support among the Japanese. We do not know the answer for sure. From an exploratory point of view, let us compare the two groups, Chinese and Japanese. The Japanese occupy a higher socio-economic status than the Chinese; in fact, the Japanese are even higher than the British on education and income indicators. The income equality is less among Japanese compared to the Chinese reflected by the Gini concentration ratios presented in Table 2.8. The Japanese are also employed in higher status occupations. Above all, they are better adapted to the host culture partly because of better socio-economic status, partly because of historical factors, and partly because of their longer stay in Canada. It may be because of these factors, in combination with others, such as their native culture, that they are able to achieve smaller family sizes much earlier than the Chinese hope to achieve in the future. To compare family sizes, we use the results of chapter 3 instead of chapter 5 because, in chapter 3, the entire population of the two groups is considered. Second, in chapter 5, we used ever-married women as the unit of analysis rather than currently married women. In chapter 3, we saw that the Japanese maintain family sizes as low as 2.33 compared to 2.55 by the Chinese. Hence, any further drastic reduction in Japanese family sizes is hard to imagine in this framework because they have already achieved relatively high socio-economic status. On the other hand, for the Chinese, there seems to be more scope for further reduction in family sizes to improve their socio-economic status.

We recognize that many questions still are to be answered. The possible questions and answers that arise from this study will be discussed in the next chapter. Some implications of the findings for further research will also be addressed. As a concluding remark to this chapter, we may say that family size differentials among the Oriental ethnic groups in Canada are partly explained through the minority group status hypothesis. The effect of this hypothesis is regarded as resulting from the interplay between structural and cultural assimilation, which reflects social and psychological insecurities. We have also shown that the history and traditions of these groups are important domains of their fertility explanation. This is an important addition to test the theory of minority group status. In the past, researchers have failed to take into account historical factors that produce fluctuations in fertility. Rindfuss and Sweet (1977) have successfully shown that, since 1920, the dominant reason for the black-white fertility differential in the United States involves historical factors. If this is any indication, we have made progress in not only being specific enough to test the theory of minority group status but also taking into account the social, cultural, and historical context within which current minority-majority fertility differentials exist.

6
Summary and Conclusions

The main focus of this research has been the development and study of Asian ethnic fertility differentials in the multi-ethnic society of Canada. Also, the focus has been the description and explanation of the effects of the socio-historical background of these ethnic groups on fertility. We were interested not only in studying the extent and nature of the fertility behaviour differentials among the three major ethnic groups (Chinese, Japanese, and East Indians) but also in investigating how the minority-status or characteristics hypotheses, originally formulated mainly in the context of the United States, might be used to explain differentials in Asian ethnic fertility in Canada. The characteristics hypothesis predicts that, as the minority group assumes the socio-economic status of the majority, fertility differentials will disappear. The minority-status hypothesis argues that, even after the minority has achieved the socio-economic status of the majority, fertility differences will exist.

In some respects, this study has been exploratory in nature. Hence, the early part of this book is devoted to providing the historical background characteristics of the Asians in Canada. This is followed by a presentation of the socio-economic background characteristics of the groups. This exposition of background information regarding the ethnic groups was helpful to delineate our expectations regarding fertility. Further, these expected differences in family sizes, delineated by our formulation, are examined first of all from the point of view of Asian ethnic group differences. Finally, Asian ethnic fertility differences are compared with the British majority to discover any departure from the majority pattern.

Two data sources were used for the study: special unpublished cross-tabulations from the 1971 census obtained from Statistics Canada and the 1971 public use sample tapes, one in one-hundred individual files. The two types of data sets dictated the type of analyses carried out. The unpublished data were used mostly for bivariate and trivariate

analyses. We started by describing the bivariate relationships between a selected set of fertility-related variables.

The bivariate analysis was used for chapters 4 and 5,
which examined the minority group status perspective as the
theoretical background for the study. The application of this
theoretical perspective to explain the Asian ethnic groups'
family size differences was achieved by using the Public Use
Sample Tapes supplemented by special tabulations that were
obtained from Statistics Canada.

6.1   SUMMARY OF FINDINGS

In 1981, there were 3,867,160 foreign-born persons in
Canada amounting to 16.1 percent of the Canadian population.
Out of this, Asians constituted 14.3 percent of all the
foreign-born persons in Canada. In other words, Asia has been
a major source of recent immigrants to Canada. The 1981
census figures indicate that there are more Asians (603,475)
than native people (491,000) in Canada. Yet, there is no
systematic demographic study of these immigrants. Particularly, no research has been done in regard to their fertility
behaviour, mortality and morbidity conditions, and migration
patterns. This may be partly because published data by Asian
ethnic origin is not available except for the Chinese and
Japanese. To bridge this gap, at least to some extent,
special tabulations were obtained from Statistics Canada to
establish socio-economic differentials among the Asian ethnic
groups. Once the socio-economic differences have been
observed, it is possible to interpret the family size differences. The remainder of the study dealt with fertility
differentials and their explanation.

In chapter 2, we began with the historical review of
Asian origin groups to understand their background in Canada.
This understanding is relevant for the study of fertility
patterns of Asian groups. Researchers in the United States
have shown that since World War II there have been large,
unprecedented, and unpredicted changes in fertility behaviour
within every social, economic, and racial group. They have
also shown that these changes cannot be accounted for by
changes in the composition of the population and that the
explanation must be linked to historical events (Rindfuss
et al., 1978).

The historical review reveals the unique experience of
each of the ethnic groups considered. The review, divided
into two parts, is organized topically and chronologically.
The first part, a review of the literature from the late
nineteenth century to the beginning of World War II, showed
how immigration policies have contributed to certain trends in
Asian immigration to Canada. Before World War II, the aspirations and particular needs of these minorities were generally
disregarded. Asian groups in Canada have suffered an imposed
invisibility--a form of denial or rejection which at best

locates them outside or below the majority norm as well as the majority priorities, interests, belief systems, and values, making them different from whatever is viewed as typically Canadian. Several episodes of socio-economic unrest (e.g., the anti-Oriental riots in Vancouver in September 1907) erupted into protest demonstrations when the majority group attempted to get rid of minorities. Although the federal government acknowledged the useful role that Asians played in the labour force, it appeared that the government had never intended for them to become real citizens or to participate in government. They were available for exploitation and then discarded. The predominant concept developed in this epoch to explain the pre-World War II experience of Asians was that of racist ideology.

The subject of immigration as an aspect of Canadian history was beginning to change in the post-World War II period. The racial discriminatory policies were abolished in favour of criteria involving education and occupational skills. In 1967, the government of Canada introduced the points system for admission of prospective immigrants. The number of immigrants the government deems appropriate to admit is determined on the basis of demographic and economic considerations. This has facilitated a shift in immigration from Europeans to Asians because of their skills and potential contribution to the Canadian economy.

The second section of chapter 2 concentrated on the bivariate analysis of a selected set of fertility-related variables. Before this, we presented the age and sex composition of the Asians by their residential status. An important observation here was that Asians are concentrated mostly in metropolitan areas, especially the recent arrivals. The reason for this concentration appears to be the availability of the occupational opportunities for which they are suited. It is also easier for these immigrants to adjust to the urban and industrial environment since they come from that type of background.

In comparing the socio-economic characteristics, we found that the Chinese as a group, compared to the Japanese and the Indians, are less educated, work in lower paid jobs, and earn substantially less. By contrast, the Indians are at the other end of the scale, and the Japanese hold intermediate positions with respect to these characteristics. This is, in fact, related to their historical background. A substantial number of Indians are recent immigrants who were selected on the basis of their educational levels and occupational skills. A very high proportion of males (40 percent compared to 16 percent of the Chinese and 15 percent of the Japanese) and females (30 percent compared to 8 percent of the Chinese and 8 percent of the Japanese) have university degrees, and thus their average annual income is also higher. Since the East Indians are more homogenized in their educational background and recency of immigration, they exhibit lower income inequality as shown by Gini concentration ratios. As far as assimilation is concerned, the Japanese are more assimilated than the other two groups. Most of the Japanese use the English language at home. This is, of course, correlated with their duration of stay in Canada. Unlike the Chinese and East Indians, very few of the Japanese are recent immigrants to Canada. For instance, less than 25 percent of the Japanese are post-war immigrants, and the rest are Canadian born. More than 75 percent of the Chinese and the East Indians are post-war immigrants, and a large proportion immigrated to Canada between 1967 and 1971.

The fact that there are historical and socio-economic differences among Asian-origin groups in Canada suggested that it is possible to expect family size differences among the groups. This was in fact demonstrated in chapter 3. There are family size differences even after controlling for both age and age at marriage. The average family size was much smaller for the East Indians, followed by the Japanese and the Chinese. However, when a control was introduced for age, the Japanese showed lower family sizes than the East Indians and the Chinese. This was not true when age at marriage was controlled. The changing positions of the Japanese and the East Indians required simultaneous control of age and age at marriage. When this was done, the Japanese showed lower fertility compared to the East Indians, especially at the older age groups. On the other hand, the Chinese consistently maintained the higher family sizes compared to the other two groups. The historical and socio-economic characteristics were found, for the most part, to be related to fertility in a manner consistent with a modernization hypothesis-namely, the more modern the background characteristics, the more modern the fertility behaviour. We also found that the differentials in fertility behaviour between the Japanese and the East Indians are indicative of the younger age structure of the East Indian women who have shorter marital duration. But what is important for our study is that controlling for these demographic factors does not remove the ethnic differences. This was well supported by our later analysis, including parity progression ratios and a life table approach. It also was shown, using the decomposition procedure, that the age structure was more important than the age at marriage for the family size difference among the groups.

The last section of the chapter dealt with the analysis of fertility and nativity. Based on the analysis, we concluded that along with nativity effects, socio-economic differences and historical factors play important roles in differentiating fertility behaviour. The most important finding of this analysis was that, unlike previous research where foreign-born women showed lower fertility than the native born, we found that the Canadian-born Asian women experience lower fertility in relation to the foreign born, especially those born in China. We attributed this to a reflection of socio-psychological insecurities. As couples experience upward mobility, they make sacrifices in family size in order to achieve and maintain expected levels of socio-economic status. This is the underlying proposition used by the minority group status hypothesis to explain ethnic fertility differentials. It is for this reason that the remaining part of this book dealt with the development and application of the minority group status hypothesis to explain Asian ethnic family size differences.

The aim of chapter 4 was to review the literature on minority group status and fertility and evaluate its adequacy as an alternative to the characteristics hypothesis. The review of literature indicated a certain inconsistency in results where the minority group status hypothesis was used to explain ethnic fertility differentials. It was suggested that the cause of this inconsistency lies in the way in which the minority-status hypothesis is used in the literature. Much of the research in the past on ethnic fertility differentials was concerned with trying to explain any observed variations in fertility between the majority group and minority populations by socio-economic factors and, if they could, not the remaining variation was attributed to the minority status of the ethnic groups. The validity of this residual explanation as a net minority status effect on fertility is questioned in this study. In the past, the support or non-support for the hypothesis was often based on how the groups were classified. In other words, the theory is based on poor conceptualization and lack of direct measurements of the concepts involved. A careful and detailed classification of minority groups is necessary in order to avoid inconsistent patterns of minority group fertility across minority groups relative to the majority group. For the socio-psychological interpretation to be convincing, it would be necessary to measure these attributes directly. To be specific, the source of the fertility differentials would have to be sought in values, beliefs, and practices peculiar to the minority groups in question.

In an attempt to revise the theory, new concepts, such as "ascribed" minority status versus "perceived" minority status were introduced. The ascribed minority status refers to a group that is a numerical minority; perceived minority status refers to a minority exhibiting greater ethnic identity, maintaining intragroup interactions, and, having faith in common beliefs and specialized institutions. Measurements of these defined concepts, through occupational and residential segregation, indicate the degree of one's minority status and ethnic integration vis-a-vis the majority society. This revision of the theory also contains the distinction between the two explanations: one explaining reduced minority fertility as a reaction to external structural pressures and another explaining high minority fertility in terms of subcultural norms and values. This distinction is very useful in accounting for any minority fertility variation, whether above or below average. More important, we have also indicated the procedure of measuring the key theoretical concept involved in the theory--marginality--based on social mobility and acculturation indicators, which are easy to obtain from simple census type data. This can avoid the usual situation where the hypothesis is tested based on indirect measurement via residuals, and thus where in choice of explanations is ad hoc.

In chapter 5, we attempted to apply the revised minority group status theory to explain the Asian ethnic fertility differentials. Since the theory required a multivariate analysis, the special cross-tabulations obtained from Statistics Canada could not be used. Instead, we used the public use sample tapes which provide micro-data on these groups. Unfortunately, such data are published only for the Chinese and the Japanese; the East Indian category had to be omitted from the analysis.

As elaborated in chapter 5, we measured the concepts of ascribed and perceived minority status by constructing the indices of residential segregation and occupational concentrations for the Chinese and Japanese. Based on these indices, we concluded that the Chinese are more ethnically integrated among themselves, indicating that their degree of perception of themselves as members of a minority is probably higher than the Japanese. Both groups do consciously think of themselves as minority groups in Canada. In addition to this, we also measured their marginal position in the Canadian society, which is also an important aspect of minority group status explanation. The findings based on this measurement are consistent with the above. The Japanese are more assimilated than the Chinese both structurally and culturally. Hence, the Chinese probably feel more marginal in the dominant society than do the Japanese.

The above findings were key to formulating our research hypothesis more specifically. Since neither of the groups have strong pronatalist norms, it is hypothesized that both of the groups seek socio-economic mobility and acculturation. The insecurities presumably associated with minority group membership should lower fertility compared with that of British majority, net of any compositional differences. In chapter 2, we observed that the Chinese have lower scores on the socio-economic variables. Moreover, in the above paragraph, we saw that the Chinese are more integrated and less acculturated; therefore, we expect stronger support for the minority group status hypothesis for the Chinese. In other words, larger reduction in family size among Chinese women is expected compared to the Japanese as a result of minority status effect.

Two special types of multiple regression analyses were used to investigate the influence of the already established minority status on fertility behaviour. The objective was to test whether the patterns of fertility differentials that occur by socio-economic status within each ethnic group still appear when all other factors of relevance are controlled. In both types of analyses, children ever born was used as our key dependent variable to measure fertility.

The first type of analysis consisted of a comparison of an additive model with that of the interaction model. We defined interaction terms in the model by linking ethnicity to the key measure of socio-economic status--in this case, education. That is, the significant interaction between ethnicity and education means that, after controlling for socio-economic and demographic characteristics (i.e., additive model), the fertility of the ethnic group differs from that of the majority at both the upper and lower social class levels. That is, minority fertility can be lower than that of the majority at the upper socio-economic levels and higher at the lower socio-economic levels (one alternative) or the reverse (second alternative). Statistically, this result is achieved by comparing the additive model to the one involving interaction terms and testing the difference in variances explained (R^2) between the two models. The significant increase in explained variance in the interaction model implies that there is an independent effect of minority group status on the fertility of the Chinese and the Japanese women. However, we could not identify the relative strength of the hypothesis in the two groups.

The second type of analysis is based on decomposing family size differences between each minority group and the majority into parts on the basis of interaction and differences in average levels of compositional variables. Since the decomposition technique we employed provides a quantitative estimate of each of these effects, their relative importance can be determined. The analysis of results obtained by the decomposition procedure has shown that the minority group status hypothesis was strongly supported among the Chinese but received relatively weaker support among the Japanese. More precisely, the independent effect of minority status of the Chinese serves to reduce fertility by more than one child whereas for Japanese it is about 0.4 child. This is what we expected based on their historical experience and socio-economic characteristics. Among the Chinese, the higher ethnic integration implies that the group membership is a dominant factor to which the effects of other variables are subordinate. These findings are consistent with the historical background of these ethnic groups, recency of immigration, and socio-economic status.

6.2 IMPLICATIONS FOR FURTHER RESEARCH

The results of this study must be interpreted with caution. We have had to make several assumptions with respect to empirical indicators of abstract concepts that are introduced and are involved in the theory of the minority group status hypothesis. We have assumed ethnic residential segregation and occupational specialization as empirical indicators of ascribed versus perceived minority status. As we know, there are more dimensions to these concepts. Similarly, the measure of marginality is not as precise as we would like. We did not have direct measures of this variable. Rather, we used two aspects of assimilation, cultural and structural, to decide about the marginality of the ethnic groups. The measurements of these two types of assimilation are also not complete. The indicators of cultural assimilation used were language of the home and index of endogamy. There are more dimensions to cultural assimilation, for instance, cognitive and psychological factors. The question is, to what extent do these variables reflect cultural assimilation? Similarly, indicators of structural assimilation can be questioned. To extend the analysis, it would be essential that the key theoretical concepts such as insecurity, marginality, and discrimination variables be directly measured and evaluated as to their influence on ethnic group fertility in the context of assimilation and minority status. Moreover, further research should also consider a more meaningful measure of ethnicity than the one we employed. It ought to consider identificational aspects of "belonging" to a particular group, participation in traditions and activities, and the degree of adherence to group norms and values of the cultural group.

In the discussion of the minority group status hypothesis and its application to the Asian ethnic groups in Canada, in addition to the social, cultural, and historical context in which ethnic fertility differentials are studied, the establishment of differential opportunity structure merits further development and investigation. It is our contention that the use of opportunity structure is more relevant for a minority group; the groups may behave differently depending on the opportunity structures. More important, the establishment of the differential opportunity structure and/or the perception of differential opportunity among the minority members may provide a link between the minority group status hypothesis and the theory of relative deprivation, as both of these concepts are invoked by different investigators to explain a basically similar phenomenon of different fertility among groups of people (see Tan, 1981 for a detailed discussion and Young, 1979 for a successful attempt to explain differential fertility in Taiwan by use of the theory of relative deprivation). Perhaps this could provide the middle range theory of the sort Merton (1957) examined if these two hypotheses, evolving from different research interests, could be brought together (Tan, 1981).

Ideally speaking, time-series or longitudinal data are required for testing the characteristics and minority group status hypotheses. The current socio-economic status of the group is irrelevant to study the past fertility experience, unless we accept the assumption that the initial members of a minority group to attain high socio-economic status are representative of all members of that group who will eventually attain a higher socio-economic status.

As we already indicated, the statistical modeling might be improved by including more fertility variables that are

directly related to fertility behaviour, and also by incor-
porating new and advanced techniques, such as simultaneous
equation causal techniques, two-stage least squares for
nonrecursive models, to handle the longitudinal approach.
These techniques would also allow us to consider some time
order between variables. Moreover, the theoretical formulation must precede the actual data collection so that more
appropriate measures can be obtained (Tan, 1981).

We realize that in social science it is often difficult
to have an ideal situation or appropriate data for investigation. Ironically, it is the data availability that most
often dictates the type of methodology that is to be used. In
spite of these limitations, we have shown how socio-
psychological attributes can be measured and modeled as
intervening variables in applying the minority group status
hypothesis to the study of Asian ethnic fertility
differentials.

References

Ahdab-Yehia, May, 1977. "Women, Employment, and Fertility Trends in the Arab Middle East and North Africa," pp. 172-87, in Stanley Kupinsky (ed.), *The Fertility of Working Women: A Synthesis of International Research.* New York: Praeger.

Alba, Richard D., 1976. "Social Assimilation Among American Catholic National-Origin Groups." *American Sociological Review* 41(6):1030-46.

Anderson, Grace, and T. L. Christie, 1978. "Ethnic Networks: North American Perspectives." *Connections* 2:25-34.

Anderson, Alan B., and James S. Frideres, 1980. *Ethnicity in Canada: Theoretical Perspectives.* Toronto: Butterworth and Co., Ltd.

Balakrishnan, T. R., 1976. "Ethnic Residential Segregation in the Metropolitan Areas of Canada." *Canadian Journal of Sociology* 1(4):481-98.

Balakrishnan, T. R., 1982. "Changing Patterns of Ethnic Residential Segregation in the Metropolitan Areas of Canada." *The Canadian Review of Sociology and Anthropology* 19(1):92-110.

Balakrishnan, T. R., J. F. Kantner, and J. D. Allingham, 1975. *Fertility and Family Planning in a Canadian Metropolis.* Montreal and London: McGill-Queen's University Press.

Balakrishnan, T. R., G. E. Ebanks, and C. F. Grindstaff, 1979. *Patterns of Fertility in Canada, 1971.* Ottawa: Statistics Canada.

Banton, Michael, 1967. *Race Relations*. New York: Basic Books, Inc.

Barelson, Bernard, 1978. "Ethnicity and Fertility: What and So What?" pp. 78-118, in Milton Himmelfarb and Victor Baras (eds.), *Zero Population Growth--For Whom?* Westport, Conn.: Greenwood Press.

Barth, F., 1969. *Ethnic Groups and Boundaries*. Boston: Little, Brown.

Basavarajappa, K. G., and S. S. Halli, 1984. "Ethnic Fertility Differences in Canada, 1926-71: An Examination of Assimilation Hypothesis." *Journal of Biosocial Science* 16(1):45-54.

Bean, Frank D., Ruth M. Cullen, Elizabeth H. Stephen, and C. Garry Swicegood, 1984. "Generational Differences in Fertility among Mexican Americans: Implications for Assessing the Effects of Immigration." *Social Science Quarterly* 65(June):573-82.

Bean, Frank D., and John P. Marcum, 1978. "Differential Fertility and the Minority Group Status Hypothesis: An Assessment and Review," pp. 189-211, in Frank D. Bean and W. Parker Frisbie (eds.), *The Demography of Racial and Ethnic Groups*. New York: Academic Press.

Beaujot, R. P., 1978. "Canada's Population: Growth and Dualism." *Population Bulletin* 33(2).

Beaujot, Roderic Paul, 1975. *"Ethnic Fertility Differentials in Edmonton."* Ph.D. diss., University of Alberta.

Beaujot, Roderic P., Karol J. Krotki, and P. Krishnan, 1977. "The Effect of Assimilation on Ethnic Fertility Differentials." Paper presented at the annual meeting of the Population Association of America. St. Louis, Missouri.

Beaujot, Roderic P., K. J. Krotki, and P. Krishnan, 1982. "Analysis of Ethnic Fertility Differentials through the Consideration of Assimilation." *The International Journal of Comparative Sociology* 23(1-2):62-70.

Beaujot, R. P., and Kevin McQuillan, 1982. *Growth and Dualism: The Demographic Development of Canadian Society*. Agincourt: Gage Educational Publishing Ltd.

Beck, Brenda E. F., 1980. "Asian Immigrants and Canadian Multiculturalism: Current Issues and Future Opportunities," pp. 1-12, in K. Victor Ujimoto and Gordon Hirabayashi (eds.), *Visible Minorities and Multiculturalism: Asians in Canada*. Toronto: Butterworth and Co., Ltd.

Bercovici, Konrad, 1923. "The Greatest Jewish City in the World." *Nation* (September 12):261.

Birdsall, Nancy, 1976. "Women and Population Studies." *Signs* 1(3):699-712.

Blake, Judith, 1968. "Are Babies Consumer Durables?: A Critique of the Economic Theory of Reproductive Motivation." *Population Studies* 22:5-25.

Blalock, Hubert M., Jr., 1966. *Toward a Theory of Minority Group Relations*. New York: Capricorn Books.

Blau, Peter M., 1964. *Exchange and Power in Social Life*. New York: Wiley.

Bogardus, E. S., 1928. *Immigration and Race Attitudes*. New York: Heath.

Boggs, Theodore H., 1923. "Oriental Immigration." *Annals of the American Academy of Political and Social Science* CVII(May):50-55.

Boggs, Theodore H., 1926. "The Oriental on the Pacific Coast." *Queen's Quarterly* 33(1-3):311-24.

Bongaarts, John, and R. G. Potter, 1983. *Fertility, Biology, and Behaviour*. New York: Academic Press.

Bowerman, Jennifer K., 1980. "East Indians in Alberta: A Human Rights Viewpoint," pp. 181-92, in K. Victor Ujimoto and Gordon Hirabayashi (eds.), *Visible Minorities and Multiculturalism: Asians in Canada*. Scarborough: Butterworth and Co., Ltd.

Browning, Harley L., 1975. "The Reproductive Behaviour of Minority Groups in the U.S.A.," in William Montagna and William A. Sadler (eds.), *Reproductive Behaviour*. New York: Plenum Publishing.

Burch, Thomas K., 1966. "The Fertility of North American Catholics: A Comparative Overview." *Demography* 3(1): 174-87.

Burch, Thomas K., 1979. "The Structure of Demographic Action." *Journal of Population* 2(4):279-93.

180 References

Burch, Thomas K., 1980. *Demographic Behavior: Interdisciplinary Perspectives on Decision-making.* Boulder, Colo.: Westview Press, Inc.

Chamie, Joseph, 1976. *"Religious Fertility Differentials in Lebanon."* Ph.D. diss., University of Michigan.

Charles, Enid, 1948. *The Changing Size of the Family in Canada.* Census Monograph No. 1. Ottawa: Queen's Printer.

Cheng, Tien-Fang, 1931. *Oriental Immigration in Canada.* Shanghai: The Commercial Press, Ltd.

Chimbos, Peter, and Carol Agocs, 1983. "Kin and Hometown Network as Support Systems for the Immigration and Settlement of Greek Canadians." *Canadian Ethnic Studies* XV(2):42-56.

China Review, 1923. "Editorial in the China Review." May: 209.

Clement, Wallace, 1975. *The Canadian Corporate Elite: An Analysis of Economic Power.* Ottawa: McClelland and Stewart, Ltd.

Coale, Ansley J., 1969. "The Decline of Fertility in Europe from the French Revolution to World War II," pp. 3-24, in S. J. Behrman, Leslie Corsa, Jr., and Ronald Freedman (eds.), *Fertility and Family Planning: A World View.* Ann Arbor: The University of Michigan Press.

Coale, A. J., 1971. "Age Patterns of Marriage." *Population Studies* 25(2):193-214.

Coale, A. J., and Paul Demeny, 1966. *Regional Model Life Tables and Table Populations.* Princeton: Princeton University Press.

Coale, A. J., and T. J. Trussell, 1974. "Model Fertility Schedules: Variations in the Age Structure of Child-bearing in Human Populations." *Population Index* 40(2): 185-258.

Coleman, J. C., Z. D. Blum, A. Sorensen, and P. H. Rossi, 1972. "White and Black Careers During the First Decade of Labour Force Experience." *Social Science Research* 1(September):243-70.

Collishaw, N. E., 1976. *Fertility in Canada: Profile Studies in 1971 Census of Canada.* Catalogue 99-706, 5 Part: (Bulletin 5:1-6) (May). Ottawa: Statistics Canada.

Darroch, G., and N. G. Marston, 1971. "The Social Class Basis of Ethnic Residential Segregation: The Canadian Case." *American Journal of Sociology* 77:491-510.

Davis, Kingsley, 1955. "Institutional Favouring High Fertility in Underdeveloped Areas." *Eugenics Quarterly* 2(March):33-39.

Davis, Kingsley, 1963. "The Theory of Change and Response in Modern Demographic History." *Population Index* 29(October):345-66.

Davis, Kingsley, and Judith Blake, 1956. "Social Structure and Fertility: An Analytic Framework." *Economic Development and Cultural Change* 4(3):211-35.

Day, Lincoln H., 1968. "Nativity and Ethnocentrism: Some Relationships Suggested by an Analysis of Catholic-Protestant Differentials." *Population Studies* 22:27-50.

Driedger, Leo, and Jacob Peters, 1977. "Identity and Social Distance: Towards Understanding Simmels The Stranger." *Canadian Review of Sociology and Anthropology* 14:158-73.

Duncan, Beverly, and O. D. Duncan, 1968. "Minorities and the Process of Stratification." *American Sociological Review* 33(June):356-64.

Easterlin, Richard A., 1975. "An Economic Framework for Fertility Analysis." *Studies in Family Planning* 6(3): 54-63.

Elliot, Jean L. (ed.), 1971. *Minority Canadians*. Scarborough: Prentice Hall of Canada.

Encyclopedia Canadiana, 1970. "People of East Indian Origin." Vol. 2:331-32 Toronto: Grolier of Canada.

Fishbein, Martin, 1972. "Toward an Understanding of Family Planning Behaviours." *Journal of Applied Social Psychology* (2-3):214-27.

Frisbie, Parker W., and Frank D. Bean, 1978. "Some Issues in the Demographic Study of Racial and Ethnic Populations," pp. 1-14, in Frank D. Bean and W. Parker Frisbie (eds.), *The Demography of Racial and Ethnic Groups*. New York: Academic Press.

Freedman, Ronald, 1963. "Norms for Family Size in Underdeveloped Areas." *Proceedings of the Royal Society* 159:220-40.

Freedman, Ronald, 1975. *The Sociology of Human Fertility: An Annotated Bibliography*. New York: Irvington.

Freedman, Ronald, P. K. Whelpton, and A. S. Campbell, 1959. *Family Planning, Sterility, and Population Growth*. New York: McGraw-Hill.

Gittler, Joseph B., 1956. *Understanding Minority Groups*. New York: John Wiley and Sons.

Glass, David V., 1968. "Fertility Trends in Europe Since the Second World War." *Population Studies* 22(March):103-46.

Glazer, Nathan, and Daniel P. Moynihan, 1975. *Ethnicity: Theory and Experience*. Cambridge: Harvard University Press.

Goldberg, David, 1975. "Socio-economic Theory and Differential Fertility: The Case of the LDC's." *Social Forces* 54(1):84-106.

Goldscheider, Calvin, 1971. *Population, Modernization, and Social Structure*. Boston: Jay-Little Co. Ltd.

Goldscheider, C., and P. R. Uhlenberg, 1969. "Minority Group Status and Fertility." *American Journal of Sociology* 74(4):361-72.

Gordon, Milton M., 1978. *Human Nature, Class, and Ethnicity*. New York: Oxford University Press.

Grabb, E. G., 1982. "Social Stratification." Chapter 6 in J. J. Teevan (ed.), *Introduction to Sociology: A Canadian Focus*. Toronto: Prentice-Hall.

Granovetter, M., 1974. *Getting a Job*. Cambridge, Mass.: Harvard University Press.

Guest, A. M., and J. Weed, 1976. "Ethnic Residential Segregation: Patterns of Change." *American Journal of Sociology* 81(5):1088-1111.

Gurak, D. T., 1980. "Assimilation and Fertility: A Comparison of Mexican American and Japanese American Women." *Hispanic Journal of Behavior Sciences* 2(September):219-39.

Halli, S. S., 1983. "Compulsory Birth Control and Fertility Measures in India: A Simulation Approach." *Simulation & Games* 14(4):429-44.

Hawkins, F., 1972. *Canada and Immigration: Public Policy and Public Concern*. Montreal: McGill, Queen's University Press.

Hawthorn, Jeoffrey, 1970. *The Sociology of Fertility*. Toronto: The MacMillan Company.

Hansen, Marcus L., 1938. "The Problem of the Third Generation Immigrant." *Augustan Historical Society Publications*, Rock Island.

Hechter, Michael, 1978. "Group Formation and the Cultural Division of Labour." *American Journal of Sociology* 84(2):293-318.

Henripin, Jacques, 1972. *Trends and Factors of Fertility in Canada*. Ottawa: Statistics Canada.

Henry, L., 1961. "Fecondite et Famille: Modeles mathematiques." *Population* 16(1):27-48.

Hoffman, L. W., and M. L. Hoffman, 1973. "The Value of Children to Parents," pp. 16-76, in J. T. Fawcett (ed.), *Psychological Perspectives on Population*. New York: Basic Books.

Homans, G. C., 1974. *Social Behaviour: Its Elementary Forms*, revised edition. New York: Harcourt Brace Jovanovich.

Hurd, B. W., 1937. "The Decline in Canadian Birth Rate." *The Canadian Journal of Economics and Political Science* 3(1):40-57.

Indra, Dorren M., 1980. "Changes in Canadian Immigration Patterns Over the Past Decade with Special Reference to Asia," pp. 163-80, in K. V. Ujimoto and Gordon Hirabayashi (eds.), *Visible Minorities and Multiculturalism: Asians in Canada*. Toronto: Butterworth and Co., Ltd.

Jaffe, A. J., Ruth M. Cullen, and Thomas D. Boswell, 1980. *The Changing Demography of Spanish Americans*. New York: Academic Press.

Jain, Sushil Kumar, 1971. *East Indians in Canada*. R.E.M.P. Bulletin, supplement 9. The Hague: Research Group for European Migration Problems.

Jiobu, R., and H. Marshall, 1977. "Minority Status and Family Size: A Comparison of Explanations." *Population Studies* 31(3):509-17.

Johnson, Nan E., 1979. "Minority Group Status and Fertility of Black Americans, 1979: A New Look." *American Journal of Sociology* 84(6):1386-1400.

Johnson, Nan E., and Ryoko Nishida, 1980. "Minority Group Status and Fertility: A Study of Japanese and Chinese in Hawaii and California." *American Journal of Sociology* 86(3):496-511.

Jones, Frank, 1967. "Ethnic Concentration and Assimilation: An Australian Case." *Social Forces* 45:412-23.

Kage, Joseph, 1967. "The Recent Changes in Canadian Immigration Regulations." *The International Migration Review* 4(Fall):47-50.

Kalbach, W. E., 1970. *The Impact of Immigration on Canada's Population*. 1961 census monograph. Ottawa: The Queen's Printer.

Kalbach, Warren E., and Wayne W. McVey, 1979. *The Demographic Bases of Canadian Society*. Toronto: McGraw Hill Company of Canada Ltd.

Kendall, Sir Maurice, 1976. *Some Notes on Statistical Problems Likely to Arise in the Analysis of W.F.S. Surveys*. World Fertility Survey Technical Bulletin No.1/TECH.441. The Hague: International Statistical Institute.

Kennedy, R. E., Jr., 1973. "Minority Group Status and Fertility: The Irish." *American Sociological Review* 38(1):85-96.

Kerlinger, Fred N., and Elazar J. Pedhazur, 1973. *Multiple Regression in Behavioural Research*. New York: Holt, Rinehart and Winston.

Kirk, Dudley, 1967. "Factors Affecting Moslem Natality," pp. 199-254, in *Proceedings of the World Population Conference, Belgrade, 1965*. New York: United Nations.

Kohn, Melvin, 1969. *Class and Conformity: A Study of Values*, 2nd Edition. Chicago: University of Chicago Press.

Komarovsky, Morra, 1964. *Blue Collar Marriage*. New York: Random House.

Krauter, Joseph F., and Morris Davis, 1978. *Minority Canadians--Ethnic Groups*. Toronto: Methuen.

Krotki, Karol J., and E. Lapierre, 1968. "La Fecondete au Canada, Selon Le Religion, L'origine Ethnique et L'etat Matrimonial." *Population* 83:815-34.

Lai, Cheun-Yan David, 1980. "The Population Structure of North American Chinatowns in the Mid-Twentieth Century: A Case Study," pp. 13-22, in K. V. Ujimoto and Gordon Hirabayashi (eds.), *Visible Minorities and Multiculturalism: Asians in Canada*. Toronto: Butterworth and Co., Ltd.

Laumann, E., 1973. *Bonds of Pluralism*. New York: Wiley.

Lee, E. S., 1966. "A Theory of Migration." *Demography* 3(1):47-57.

Li, Peter S., 1979. "An Historical Approach to Ethnic Stratification: The Case of Chinese in Canada, 1858-1930." *Canadian Review of Sociology and Anthropology* 16:320-32.

Li, Peter S., 1980. "Income Achievement and Adaptive Capacity: An Empirical Comparison of Chinese and Japanese in Canada," pp. 363-78, in K. V. Ujimoto and Gordon Hirabayashi (eds.), *Visible Minorities and Multiculturalism: Asians in Canada*. Toronto: Butterworth and Co., Ltd.

Li, Peter S., 1982. "Chinese Immigrants on the Canadian Prairie, 1919-48." *Canadian Review of Sociology and Anthropology* 19(4):527-40.

Lieberson, Stanley, 1963. "The Old-New Distinction and Immigrants in Australia." *American Sociological Review* 28(4):550-65.

Lieberson, Stanley, 1970. *Language and Ethnic Relations in Canada*. New York: John Wiley and Sons.

Lingoes, James C., 1973. *The Grittman-Lingoes Nonmetric Program Series*. Ann Arbor: Mahesis Press.

Lopez, D. E., and G. Sabagh, 1978. "Untangling Structural and Normative Aspects of the Minority Status - Fertility Hypothesis." *American Journal of Sociology* 83(6): 1491-97.

Lunde, Anders, 1965. "White-Nonwhite Fertility Differentials in the United States." *Health, Education, and Welfare Indicators*. (September):1-16.

Marcum, John P., 1978. "The Effect of Neighbourhood Racial Composition on the Relationship Between Minority Group Status and Current Fertility." Unpublished paper.

Marcum, John P., 1980. "Comment on 'Untangling Structural Normative Aspects of the Minority Status - Fertility Hypothesis' by Lopez and Sabagh." *American Journal of Sociology* 86(2):377-81.

Marshall, H., and R. Jiobu, 1980. "A Rejoinder to Professor Burch." *Population Studies* 34(1):377.

Marston, W. G., 1969. "Social Class Segregation Within Ethnic Groups in Toronto." *Canadian Review of Sociology and Anthropology* 6:65-79.

Merton, Robert K., 1957. *Social Theory and Social Structures*. Glencoe, Ill.: The Free Press.

Mirowsky, John, and Catherine Ross, 1980. "Minority Status, Ethnic Culture, and Distress: A Comparison of Blacks, Whites, Mexicans and Mexican Americans." *American Journal of Sociology* 86(3):479-95.

Monthly Labour Review, 1927. "Orientals in British Columbia." XXIV(May):1137-40.

Morse, Eric W., 1935. *"Immigration and Status of British East Indians in Canada."* Master's thesis, Queen's University, Kingston.

Morse, Eric W., 1936. "Some Aspects of the Komagatu Maru Affair, 1914." *Canadian Historical Association*, report.

Murguia, Edward, 1975. *Assimilation, Colonialism, and the Mexican American People*. Austin, Texas: Mexican American Studies Centre, University of Texas Press.

Muthanna, I. M., 1975. *People of India in North America*. Bangalore: Lotus Printing House.

Namboodiri, Krishnan N., 1980. "A Look at Fertility Model-Building from Different Perspectives," pp. 71-90, in Thomas K. Burch (ed.), *Demographic Behaviour: Interdisciplinary Perspectives on Decision Making*. Boulder, Colo.: Westview Press, Inc.

Neter, John, and William Wasserman, 1974. *Applied Linear Statistical Models*. Homewood, Ill.: Richard Irwin Inc.

Norris, John, 1948. *Strangers Entertained: A History of the Ethnic Groups of British Columbia*. Vancouver: Evergreen.

Oppenheimer, Valerie K., 1970. *The Female Labor Force in the United States*. Berkeley: Institute of International Studies, University of California.

Outlook, LXXXIV Magazine, 1906. "Asiatic Immigration into Canada." (October):349.

Page, H. J., 1977. "Patterns Underlying Fertility Schedules: A Decomposition by Both Age and Marriage Duration." *Population Studies* 30(3):85-106.

Park, Robert E., 1928. "Human Migration and the Marginal Man." *American Journal of Sociology* 33(6):881-93.

Petersen, William, 1961. *Population*. New York: MacMillan.

Petersen, William, 1964. *The Politics of Population*. New York: Doubleday and Company.

Petersen, William, 1968. *Population*. 2nd edition. London: The MacMillan Co.

Poffenberger, Shirley B., and Thomas Poffenberger, 1975. *Fertility and Family Life in an Indian Village*. Ann Arbor: Center for South and Southeast Asian Studies, University of Michigan.

Porter, John, 1965. *The Vertical Mosaic*. Toronto: University of Toronto Press.

Pressat, R., 1972. *Demographic Analysis*. Chicago: Aldine Publishing Co.

Price, Charles A., 1963. *Southern Europeans in Australia*. Melbourne: Oxford University Press.

Pryor, Edward, and Douglas Norris, 1983. "Canada in the Eighties." *American Demographics* 15(12):25-29.

Raj, Samuel, 1980. "Some Aspects of East Indian Struggle in Canada, 1905-1947," pp. 83-90, in K. V. Ujimoto and Gordon Hirabayashi (eds.), *Visible Minorities and Multiculturalism: Asians in Canada*. Toronto: Butterworth and Co., Ltd.

Ram, Bali, 1977. "Regional Sub-Cultural Explanations of Black Fertility in the United States." *Population Studies* 30(3):553-59.

Rawlyk, George A., 1962. *Historical Essays on the Atlantic Provinces*. Toronto: McClelland and Stewart.

Reitz, J. G., 1980. *The Survival of Ethnic Groups*. Toronto: McGraw-Hill.

Rele, J. R., and Tara Kanitkar, 1976. "Fertility Differentials by Religion in Greater Bombay: Role of Explanatory Variables," pp. 371-84, in Lado T. Ruzicka (ed.), *The Economic and Social Supports for High Fertility*. Proceedings of the conference in Canberra, 16-18 November.

Richmond, Anthony H., 1972. *Ethnic Residential Segregation in Metropolitan Toronto*. Toronto: Institute for Behavioural Research, York University.

Richmond, Anthony H., and John Goldlust, 1974. "A Multivariate Model of Immigrant Adaption." *International Migration Review* 8(2):193-226.

Richmond, Anthony H., and Warren Kalbach, 1980. *Factors in the Adjustment of Immigrants and Their Descendants*. Ottawa: Statistics Canada.

Rindfuss, Ronald R., 1980. "Minority Status and Fertility Revisited--Again: A Comment on Johnson." *American Journal of Sociology* 86(2):372-75.

Rindfuss, Ronald R., John Shelton Reed, and Craig St. John, 1978. "A Fertility Reaction to a Historical Event: Southern White Birthrates and the 1954 Desegregation Ruling," pp. 213-20, in Frank D. Bean and W. Parker Frisbie (eds.), *The Demography of Racial and Ethnic Groups*. New York: Academic Press.

Rindfuss, Ronald R., and James A. Sweet, 1977. *Postwar Fertility Trends and Differentials in the United States*. New York: Academic Press.

Ritchey, P. Neal, 1975. "The Effect of Minority Groups Status on Fertility: A Re-examination of Concepts." *Population Studies* 29(2):249-57.

Ritchey, P. Neal, 1976. "Explanations of Migration." *Journal of the Royal Statistical Society* XLVII (part 2):167-227.

Roberts, R. E., and Eun Sul Lee, 1974. "Minority Group Status and Fertility Revisited." *American Journal of Sociology* 80(2):503-23.

Robinson, Warren C., and Sarah F. Harbison, 1980. "Toward a Unified Theory of Fertility," pp. 201-35, in Thomas K. Burch (ed.), *Demographic Behaviour: Interdisciplinary Perspectives on Decision-making*. Boulder, Colo.: Westview Press, Inc.

Round Table XIII Magazine, 1923. "Asiatic Immigration into Canada." (May):398-404.

Ryder, Norman B., 1973. "Recent Trends and Group Differences in Fertility," in Charles F. Westoff (ed.), *Toward the End of Growth*. Englewood Cliffs, N. J.: Prentice Hall.

Ryder, Norman B., 1982. *Progressive Fertility Analysis*. WFS Technical Bulletin no. 8. London, England.

Ryder, Norman B., and Charles F. Westoff, 1971. *Reproduction in the United States, 1965*. Princeton, N. J.: Princeton University Press.

Sampat-Mehta, R., 1973. *International Barriers*. Ottawa: Harpell's Press.

Schermerhorn, R. A., 1970. *Comparative Ethnic Relations: A Framework for Theory and Research*. New York: Random House.

Schooler, Carmi, 1976. "Serfdom's Legacy." *American Journal of Sociology* 81(May):1265-86.

Shaw, Charles Lug, 1924. "Canada's Oriental Problem." *Canada Month* LXIII(October):334-38.

Shibata, Yuko, 1980. "Coping with Values in Conflict: Japanese Women in Canada," pp. 257-76, in K. V. Ujimoto and Gordon Hirabayashi (eds.), *Visible Minorities and Multiculturalism: Asians in Canada*. Toronto: Butterworth and Co., Ltd.

Shryock, Henry S., and Jacob S. Siegel and Associates, 1973. *The Methods and Materials of Demography*. Washington, D.C. U.S.: Government Printing Office.

Sihra, Nand Singh, 1913. "Indians in Canada: A Pictorial Account of Their Hardships by One Who Comes from the Place and Knows Them." *The Modern Review* 8:140-49.

Sly, David F., 1970. "Minority-group Status and Fertility: An Extension of Goldscheider and Uhlenberg." *American Journal of Sociology* 76(11):433-59.

Stahura, John M., and Barbara T. Stahura, 1975. "Class, Minority Status and Fertility." *International Review of Modern Sociology* 5:45-59.

Stahura, John M., and Barbara Stahura, 1979. "Racial Status, Mobility Aspirations and Fertility--A Social-Psychological Test of the Minority Group Status' Hypothesis." *Journal of Comparative Family Studies* 10(1):127-30.

St. John, Craig, 1982. "Race Differences in Age at First Birth and the Pace of Subsequent Fertility: Implications for the Minority Groups Status Hypothesis." *Demography* 19(3):301-14.

Story, Norah, 1967. "Oriental Immigration," pp. 617-18, in her *The Oxford Companion to Canadian History and Literature*. Toronto: Oxford University Press.

Stycos, J. M., 1968. *Human Fertility in Latin America*. New York: Cornell University Press.

Sunahara, Ann M., 1980. "Federal Policy and the Japanese Canadians: The Decision to Educate, 1942," pp. 93-120, in K. V. Ujimoto and Gordon Hirabayashi (eds.), *Visible Minorities and Multiculturalism: Asians in Canada*. Toronto: Butterworth Co., Ltd.

Tabachnick, Barbara G., and Linda S. Fidell, 1983. *Using Multivariate Statistics*. New York: Harper and Row, Publishers.

Taeuber, K. E., and A. F. Taeuber, 1965. *Negroes in Cities*. New York: Aldine Press.

Tan, Boon-Ann, 1981. *"Fertility Differences in Peninsular Malaysia: The Ethnic Factor."* Ph.D. diss., University of Michigan, Ann Arbor.

The Canadian Family Tree: Canada's People, 1960. Multiculturalism Directorate, Department of the Secretary of State, Government Publication, Ottawa.

The Canadian Family Tree: Canada's People, 1967. Multiculturalism Directorate, Department of the Secretary of State, Government Publication, Ottawa.

The Canadian Family Tree: Canada's People, 1979. Multiculturalism Directorate, Department of the Secretary of State, Government Publication, Ottawa.

Timlin, Mabel F., 1957. "Canada's Immigration Policy, 1896-1910." *The Canadian Journal of Economics and Political Science* XXVII, 4(11):517-32.

Tracey, W. R., 1941. "Fertility of the Population of Canada." *Seventh Census of Canada*. 1931, 12(monographs):215-408.

Trovato, Frank, 1987. "A Macro Sociological Analysis of Native Indian Fertility in Canada: 1961, 1971 and 1981." *Social Forces*. Forthcoming.

Trovato, Frank, 1978. *The Relationship Between Assimilation and Ethnic Fertility in Canada: An Examination of Census Data*." Master's thesis, University of Western Ontario, London.

Trovato, Frank, and T. K. Burch, 1980. "Minority Group Status and Fertility in Canada." *Canadian Ethnic Studies* 8(3): 1-18.

Trovato, Frank, and S. S. Halli, 1983. "Ethnicity and Migration in Canada." *International Migration Review* 17(Summer):245-67.

Uhlenberg, P. R., 1973. "Fertility Patterns Within the Mexican American Population." *Social Biology* 20(March): 30-39.

Ujimoto, K. Victor, 1976. "Contrasts in the Pre-War and Post-War Japanese Community in British Columbia: Conflict and Change." *Canadian Review of Sociology and Anthropology* 13:80-89.

Ujimoto, K. Victor, and Gordon Hirabayashi (eds.), 1980. *Visible Minorities and Multiculturalism: Asians in Canada*. Toronto: Butterworth and Co., Ltd.

Vallee, Frank G., Mildred Schwartz, and Frank Darnell, 1956. "Ethnic Assimilation and Differentiation in Canada." *Canadian Journal of Economics and Political Science* 23: 540-56.

Van Heek, F., 1956. "Roman Catholicism and Fertility in the Netherhlands." *Population Studies* 10:125-38.

Verma, Ravi B. P., 1980. "Variations in Family Size Among Canadian Women by Generation and Ethnic Group." *International Journal of Comparative Sociology* XX(3-4): 293-303.

Visaria, Leela, 1974. "Religious Differentials in Fertility," pp., 361-74, in Ashish Bose, Ashok Mitra, P. B. Desai, and J. N. Sharma (eds.), *Population in India's Development 1974-2000*. Delhi: Vikas Publishing House.

Wagley, C., and M. Harris, 1959. *Minorities in the New World*. New York: Columbia University Press.

Weller, Robert H., 1977. "Wife's Employment and Cumulative Family Size in the United States, 1970 and 1960." *Demography* 14(February):43-66.

Westoff, Charles F., and Norman B. Ryder, 1971. *Reproduction in the United States, 1965*. Princeton, N. J.: Princeton University Press.

Westoff, Charles F., and Norman B. Ryder, 1977. *The Contraceptive Revolution*. Princeton, N. J.: Princeton University Press.

Whelpton, P. K., 1946. "Reproduction Rates Adjusted for Age, Partity, Fecundity, and Marriage." *Journal of the American Statistical Association* 236 (December):501-16.

Whelpton, Pascal K., Arthur Campbell, and John Patterson, 1966. *Fertility and Family Planning in the United States*. Princeton, N. J.: Princeton University Press.

Whiteley, A. A., 1931. "Immigration on the Pacific Coast." *"Current History"* magazine, *New York Times*. XXXIII(February):720-22.

Williams, J. B., 1907. "Canada's New Immigrant: The Hindu." *Canada Month* XXVIII (February):383-86.

Woodsworth, Charles James, 1937. "Canada's Oriental Immigrants." *Canadian Forum* XVII (11):268-70.

Wunsch, Guillaume J., and Marc G. Termote, 1978. *Introduction to Demographic Analysis: Principles and Methods*. New York: Plenum Press.

Yancey, W. L., E. P. Ericksen, and R. N. Juliani, 1976. "Emergent Ethnicity: A Review and Reformulation." *American Sociological Review* 41(3):391-402.

Young, Dhin Lain, 1979. *"Development Strategy, Relative Deprivation and Fertility Behaviour in Taiwan."* Ph.D. diss., University of Michigan, Ann Arbor.

Young, Charles H., and R. Y. Reid, 1938. "Oriental Standards of Living," pp. 272-92, in M. A. Innes (ed.), *The Japanese Canadians*. Toronto: University of Toronto Press.

Index

About the Author

SHIVALINGAPPA S. HALLI is Assistant Professor of Sociology at the University of Manitoba, Winnipeg, Canada. He has written extensively on demographic and minority group issues in *Rural Sociology, Population Review, International Migration Review,* and other journals.